MAGIC OF THE QUORN

ULRICA MURRAY SMITH

Magic

OF THE

Quorn

J. A. ALLEN & CO LTD
London
and New York

British Library Cataloguing in Publication Data
Magic of the Quorn.
1. Quorn
I. Title
799.2'59'744420924   SK287.G73Q/

ISBN 0–85131–362–0

Published in 1980 by
J. A. Allen & Company Limited
1 Lower Grosvenor Place
Buckingham Palace Road
London SW1W 0EL

Typeset by Inforum Ltd, Portsmouth
Printed in Great Britain by
Redwood Burn Ltd., Trowbridge
and bound by Robert Hartnoll Ltd., Bodmin

FOREWORD
by HRH PRINCE CHARLES
Prince of Wales, KG

Ulrica Murray Smith asked me to write the foreword to
this splendid book she has produced. What else could I
do? How could I possibly refuse an offer made by the
Joint Master of the Quorn . . .? In fact, it is a delight to
attempt to provide something suitable for apart from the
fact that Ulrica has been extraordinarily kind to me over
the past five years, she has also written an eminently
readable book, of just the right length, and crammed
with some of the funniest anecdotes and observations I
have read for a long time. I always think a book is a great
success if it makes you laugh out loud on more than one
occasion!

A part from chuckling my way through this book it was
also intriguing to note the changes that have taken place,
particularly with The Quorn, since those apparently
carefree and wire-free years between the two wars.
Eccentricity seemed to flourish on a grand scale, being
given every conceivable opportunity to do so. Eccentricity is still around, but the opportunities to indulge in it
are far more limited. But the magic in Leicestershire is
still there, although I must admit that it takes a little time

to appreciate it when you first go to The Quorn or The Belvoir. The great Duke of Wellington apparently used to encourage as many of his cavalry officers as possible to hunt in the Shires in order that they could acquire that particular brand of dash, fire and an eye for country which so distinguished the British cavalry in the 18th and 19th centuries. When you first visit The Quorn you can't help feeling, while being trampled in the rush, that the majority of the field are still in training for one of Wellington's campaigns! It doesn't, however, take very long to adapt to the environment – the only difficulty being to try and keep your head while others in the vicinity tend to be losing theirs! I remember on one occasion there was a frantic rush to "get forward" through a gap in a hedge and several people shouted at me in the mêlée – "push on, Sir, push on". I'm afraid my response was to maintain a strict calm and to observe that *someone* had to try and keep up the standard . . .! My view is that there is always opportunity for "dash and fire", if you have a reasonable horse, once you have got going, but displaying it in the gateway can be somewhat hazard-ous to all!

I feel sure that this book will give a great deal of pleasure to many people – especially in Leicestershire – and that it will no doubt re-awaken all sorts of memories in several minds. Who knows – it may inspire a rush of memoirs from other pens . . .? Whatever happens, I pray that Ulrica has many more years, mounted on her big horses, firmly under the spell of The Quorn's magic.

CONTENTS

ILLUSTRATIONS

1

FIRST
IMPRESSIONS

When my somewhat sketchy education had been completed and I was about to have the dubious pleasure of becoming a débutante, my father suggested taking me for a month's hunting away from home, which was on the Sussex downs.

Father was a beautiful horseman, and had been a first class polo player; he always schooled his hunters like polo ponies. He had wonderful hands and liked experimenting with different bits, of which he had an enormous collection; many I still have.

A visit to the Blackmore Vale was first discussed, as we had a cousin living there; but then fate took over – and what a difference it has made to my life!

Father met his old friend General John Vaughan, who, with his wife, was running Craven Lodge at Melton Mowbray; he suggested that we should go there. So off we went to Leicestershire. I remember my father saying that I should enjoy the Crawley and Horsham all the more after experiencing hunting in the Shires. A statement I shall always doubt, but as I never did go back except for an odd day's hunting in the spring, I shall never know for certain.

Craven Lodge had until recently been run by Mrs Vaughan's son, Mike Wardell, (who had left Leicestershire) and his wife Hilda. (Hilda had since remarried, a very amusing character called Lizzie Lezard, and they both hunted from Melton.) By all accounts it had been madly gay with the smart set all flocking there in the winter. The Princes started the fashion by having a suite there. Parties were apparently given every night, and poker played for fabulously high stakes, while gentlemen ran off only too frequently with other gentlemen's wives.

However, in my day, it was the most respectable place to stay, and very quiet, except for the odd party given there.

The accommodation may have been dull, but the hunting surpassed my wildest dreams. The Quorn, Belvoir, and Cottesmore all met within easy riding distance from Melton; you could hunt six days a week, the horses all going on by road. The country was nothing but grass, with glorious fences and timber, enabling the field to spread out and take their own line, jumping anywhere. But there was a vast crowd, and it was essential to keep wide awake to get a good start, as manners were not apparent in the first gateway or so. There was a certain knack to getting away, soon learned in the Shires, which I think strangers usually found difficult to cope with at first, as they would find themselves pushed aside.

To begin with, I must admit, some of the riders simply terrified me; they looked me up and down, making me feel that I must have my spurs on upside down or a similar misdemeanor. Fortunately, I did know that hat guards were absolutely taboo in Leicestershire, though worn at that time in the provinces, so I had not committed that error, nor did I carry a sandwich case nor flask on the saddle, which was (and is) terribly non-U.

I can remember being filled with alarm and apprehension before the first party I went to, but I found everyone more than friendly – well the men anyhow.

In the hunting field the turn-out was absolutely faultless. Gentlemen wore scarlet swallow-tail coats with white leather breeches, which they kept from getting a speck of dirt on by wearing a silk apron until they actually mounted their horse. 'Leathers' become lethal if it rains, as they are so slippery when wet, which must be a drawback, but otherwise they are warm and extremely smart.

Donnie Player and Flash Kellet, both killed in the war, Hugh Lloyd Thomas, who won the National, Jackie de Pret and Toby Greenall (now Lord Daresbury), were among others who looked the part, in silk hats, with top boots polished till they gleamed. They rode big blood horses in double bridles, with plaited manes.

Many of the ladies rode side-saddle, with beautifully cut habits, top hats, or occasionally bowlers, all with veils. Lady Fortescue was the epitome of elegance, as were Mrs Fred Cripps, Mrs Jack Harrison and Mrs Reggie Farquhar (widow of Gilbert Greenall). Lexie Wilson (later Spencer) who went very well on anything, rode astride, wearing a long greyish coat, cut like a man's. Others who rode astride mostly wore black coats and boots, with yellow breeches and bowler hats; of these Monica Sheriffe was one of the smartest, and well mounted. Olive Partidge too went well, always riding very small animals. A few ladies preferred blue coats with breeches to match, which to my mind made them look like chauffeurs.

Of course it must be remembered that all the houses were crammed with servants. No one ever thought of throwing a log on the fire, or drawing the curtains; the butler or footman would do that. A special valet was employed just to clean the hunting clothes.

My eyes were on stalks the first time I saw the second horses arrive, an army of them, led by the huntsman's second horseman, who with the master's and the whippers-in's men, wore exactly the same kit as the hunt servants, but with a spare stirrup leather over one shoulder. The other second horsemen, (all male, I never saw a second horsewoman,) wore bowler hats, hunting ties, black coats and boots, with tan breeches. They often carried sandwich cases and flasks strapped to their backs. (Not for their own consumption, but for their masters and mistresses.) The Harrison's men were the exceptions as they wore livery with top hats and cockades.

Stables were full of the most beautiful quality hunters, which had been broken, properly schooled and brought on till they were seven or eight years old before their owners ever rode them.

There were two big dealer's yards in Melton, both full of hunters. One was owned by Harry Beeby, the other by the Young brothers. They did a tremendous trade, and each employed several expert rough riders to bring on young horses, or improve the older ones. Great trouble was taken to assess their clients' capabilities and try to suit horse to rider. If the animal turned out a failure they would always exchange it, but there was a saying that if you made many exchanges you ended up with a donkey, as the dealers were rather shrewder than their clients!

In those days there were quite a number of people who hunted from Melton because it was the smart thing to do, and not necessarily because they enjoyed it. They would make an immaculate appearance at the meet, then ride around with the 'road brigade' before returning home for a late lunch. Some people crossed the country brilliantly, sometimes riding very jealously, while others looked for the gates. Some watched hounds (a few rode on them!) while others never saw one all day, but they all found fun in their fashion.

The two millionaires, Lord Furness who lived at Burrough, and Lowenstein who was at Thorpe Satchville, were no longer there when I arrived at Melton. Lord Furness had, I think, gone to live in Africa and Lowenstein had jumped out of an aeroplane. There was a splendid story of some sale of hunters to which both tycoons had sent a minion with orders to buy a certain horse. Neither of them was used to being thwarted in their wishes, and it simply had not occurred to them to mention any price, just 'buy it'. But it so happened that they had picked on the same horse. The result was that the animal was finally knocked down for the most exorbitant sum, more fitting for a Derby winner. I forget which minion lost his nerve, but I gathered that nobody was very pleased, except the seller, who as you can imagine was over the moon with delight.

The late Duke of Gloucester had a house in Melton, and the Prince of Wales (the Duke of Windsor) and Prince George both hunted fairly regularly, often staying with Lady Furness. The Prince of Wales always wore his top hat at quite an angle on the side of his head; he rode rather short, and always in a snaffle which was unusual in those days; but he went like a bomb, as does his great nephew now. His brothers rode quite well, but were rather nervous. I never saw the Duke of York, (the late King George VI); he hunted with the Pytchley, and was piloted by George Drummond, head of Drummond's Bank, who was a great character, and hunted in Leicestershire as well, and I recall jumped fantastic obstacles on an exceptional grey horse.

When my father returned to Sussex, I went to stay with Marjorie Leigh, who lived at Warwick Lodge, Melton which is now the County Council Rates Department. It was in those days a very luxurious place to stay. I remember thick white carpets, tiger skins, masses of servants, and more important a stable full of first-class horses.

Marjorie and I were to compete against one another in point to points for several seasons; as both our parents lived in Sussex, we used to race down there when our hunting was over.

Three royal brothers with the Quorn. The then
Prince of Wales (afterwards the Duke of Windsor) with the
late Duke of Gloucester and the Duke of Kent
killed on active service with the RAF

Sir Harold Nutting with huntsman George Barker

The author show jumping Lively Lord at the
City of Leicester Horse Show. August 1957

2

ROTHERBY
COTTAGE

Diana Fellowes had become a great friend of mine, she was a few years older than me, and was quite the most beautiful girl I have ever seen, both on or off a horse, and was the most charming person.

Diny and I decided to take a cottage together for the season. Her first idea was a trifle impractical, as she was mad keen for us to take 'Thimble Hall' which was at the time a derelict cottage, but as she said it sounded so chic! With a more realistic outlook, I thought the lack of proper roof, and all type of plumbing mattered more than the address.

We finally settled on Rotherby Cottage, which is near Brooksby. Anne Bridgeman, now Lady Anne Cowdray, came to join us at weekends; both she and Diny rode side saddle, looked stunning and rode extremely well. It was the happiest arrangement and a blissful year.

Just before we were to move in, I received a letter from Diny, ending 'Now as to dull domestic details – I will bring a gramophone, will you provide a backgammon board?' Unfortunately, we had failed to realise that linen was not provided with the house, however this hitch was soon rectified by a supply from Lowesby, covered in coronets. The Blandfords, (the late Duke and Duchess of Marlborough) were always very kind to us.

A friend of Diny's lent us his soldier servant, (would the War Office have approved I wonder?) and he and his wife were our 'staff'. The wife cooked breakfast for us, then we would be out hunting all day, and usually dine with friends in the evening. We did not, I am afraid, return the great hospitality we enjoyed.

We were a little short of 'tinkle' so we used to toss up before going out to dinner who would plead with our host to have petrol put in our car, making some excuse why the tank happened to be empty. The chauffeur would be sent for and the car duly filled up. It saved a lot of money – I only wish I could do it now.

We had a stable yard and three horses each, but we used to hunt every day. I soon discovered that I only had to look depressed, (which comes naturally to me) saying that I had nothing to ride, for a horse to be produced by some kind friend. Most people had far too many hunters anyway. That season I had 85 days hunting and rode 25 different horses.

The meets were at cross roads, or on the village green; lawn meets were very rare, and none of the hunts met at farms and public houses as we do today.

I think there were fewer foxes then, than at the present time. I see from an old diary of mine, that quite often we had not found a fox until two or three o'clock, or did not find again after changing horses. Perhaps that is one of the reasons why the galloping cast to the next covert became fashionable in Leicestershire. When hounds did run there was nothing to stop you, and it was heaven. No wheat or seeds, not even a ploughed field, no wire, and no cars because there were very few roads, and any lane had a gate to every field.

With the Cottesmore I suppose that Prior's Coppice and Orton Park were two of their finest coverts. In the Belvoir Sherbrooks certainly was their best, as from there you could have a good hunt in any direction, but possibly the favourite way was into Quorn country by the Broughtons. The same sort of line the other way on, with the Quorn from Curate's was lovely, and the Hoby Vale was grand to ride over. In the Quorn Friday country The Prince of Wales was undoubtedly the best covert.

The Burton Flats in the Cottesmore, bordering on the Quorn, was ideal for those not so brave, as hounds always seemed to run fast there, and the fences were tiny, although some of them had big ditches which could come as a shock to the unwary. I shall never forget one evening hunt across the Flats with the Cottesmore, when the moon was up and there was a ground mist, covering everything like a cloud. Hounds, making a tremendous cry, were quite invisible, and the few remaining riders appeared like legless Centaurs; and one hoped the fences would be big enough to appear above the cloud – it was like a weird dream and terribly exciting.

It was all very gay and social because the 'carpet baggers' as they were called, all took houses in Melton or neighbouring villages and came for the season, plus servants, horses and grooms; some even arrived by private train in October.

The people who lived in the Quorn unfashionable side, beyond Loughborough, which includes Charnwood Forest were known as 'the beasts of the forest' by the Meltonians, but they were inclined to look down on anyone who lived more than ten miles from Melton.

Diny had several men very much in love with her; I recall one incident when she had three falls in one day and on each occasion was picked up by an American, Jimmy Clarke. He admired her tremendously but had not met her until that day, so was delighted at the opportunity; but after the third time he helped her up, she smiled sweetly at him and said 'What an odd coincidence, I have had three falls, and every time an American has picked me up.' Poor Jimmy was shattered that she had not recognised him.

One night dining at Thorpe Satchville Hall with the Gerard Leighs, Diny and I found G. Leigh sitting between us; he was home for Christmas in his last year at Eton. Diny asked him if he was coming to the party the following night, he replied that he was not as he would not know anyone. Diny told him that he could dance with her, and with me, at which he looked horrified and said, 'But you are much too old.' Not quite the courtier that he is today!

We saw a good deal of Charlie Clarke, who was Bert Blandford's agent and lived at Lowesby Hall Farm; he was the most amusing character, and used to write witty but very libellous rhymes about everyone. He presented me with a cocktail shaker, which I still have, on which is inscribed,

> 'Ulrica Thynne, Diana Fellowes
> One afrights, the other mellows
> Shake the vermouth, mix the gin
> Jolly Fellowes . . . Thynne.'

I forget what I had done to incur his wrath.

Geoff Harbord used to write the Leicestershire Letter in the Tatler each week, which was more gossip than hunting; he was very clever at making it obvious to whom he was referring without mentioning names, thus saving any possibility of libel action. The Times carried hunting accounts of a rather more serious nature every day.

The summer after our Rotherby season Diny married Henry Broughton; they took Brooksby Hall for one season from Admiral Beatty, who then hunted from Dingley. Brooksby is now an Agricultural College, and the Masters of Foxhounds Association have held two of their very successful weekends of lectures and discussions there.

Soon after their Brooksby winter Diny became very ill, and although she recovered, she and Henry lived near Windsor, and spent much time in Switzerland for her health; so that Diny never hunted again, but we kept in close touch. Then at the end of '36 much to her joy, she had a son, (the present Lord Fairhaven) but she became very ill again for several months, and died when he was under a year old. It was a great tragedy as everybody loved her, and she had so much to live for.

Second Horsemen on
Guthrie hill.

3

QUENBY

Soon after Diny married, Sir Harold and Lady Nutting asked me to spend the winter at Quenby, and from then until I was married it became my second home.

Enid Nutting was the kindest person, and could be very funny – she had a fixation on illness, and it was a favourite subject with her. The only time I can think of her being cross was when she found me reading a library book, which she was convinced had brought every sort of germ into the house. I had to promise never to touch another library book.

One of the first things Enid told me was that they had enormous and very tedious lunch parties every Sunday, which turned out to be true, but that I was welcome to stay or go out as I liked, provided she knew in advance.

In 1930 Harold had joined Algy Burnaby for two years as Master of the Quorn, then he continued on his own until 1940. He was always superbly mounted, and his turn out and that of the Hunt staff was impeccable. His own horses and those for his sons were kept at Quenby, and the Hunt horses at the kennels, at Barrow-on-Soar.

A great deal of telephoning instructions and arrangements always went on the evening before hunting, but what the draw was going to be, or where we were likely to change horses or end the day was always kept a complete secret. If we were going to 'The Curate' which was my favourite covert, as a great concession Harold would tell me to ride my best horse first or second to coincide. If one of his lady friends rang up to ask where to leave her car, Harold would say firmly, 'In your garage I hope.' and ring off.

John Nutting, the eldest son, was a great friend of mine, and we went to many parties together and would compare notes on how we got on, and who we fancied, which would change from day to day. John was at Sandhurst and then joined the Scots Greys. He and Edric, who later went into the Blues, were both killed in the war. Anthony was at Eton; much later he was to become a Privy Councillor and an author, and we have always remained close friends.

After having experienced Leicestershire, and decided that the provinces were not for me, my father generously allowed me to bring not only my horses, but also his groom, Martin, with me to Melton every season to look after my horses. Martin was with me for years, and is still stud groom to my ex-husband at Gumley.

While I was staying at Quenby my hunters were stabled first at Gaddesby Hall, which belonged to Jackie de Pret, and later with Sam Ashton at Melton.

Sam was always immaculately turned out, and was full of entrancing anecdotes of people in the past. My favourite story, which I have no idea if it is true or not, took place when he was a subaltern in the Life Guards. Apparently Sam had come off guard in London and hurried up to Leicestershire in the hope of joining hounds in the late afternoon. But as it had been a very faint chance, he was dressed in 'ratcatcher', which so infuriated the master that he wrote to Sam's commanding officer complaining that an officer of the Household Cavalry had appeared out hunting improperly dressed. Sam duly received a rocket, which so annoyed him, that at his next encounter with hounds he was seen to be faultlessly turned out, but riding a cow, which had been clipped, smartly bridled and saddled, and with her hooves polished. The master evidently failed to see the funny side, another scathing letter was written, and Sam confined to barracks for a spell.

There were no cattle grids in those days, so that there were at least three gates to go through in any direction from Quenby. If I was alone I used to get out and unlatch the gate, then push it open with the car, which saved getting out twice, but was not tremendously good for the car or the gate. I was always accused of having broken the Forty Pound Gate, but as it was on the Baggrave estate, owned by the Burnabys, no one (at Quenby) minded.

Harold Nutting was always most particular that every item connected with foxhunting must be correct. If anyone spoke of 'cubbing' or the 'whip' instead of the whipper-in, he would nearly have a stroke. There are many pitfalls in speech about hunting, into which I may say even the most educated and eminent used to fall much to Harold's disdain.

Harold used to say how he would love to have a private pack, only asking his friends to hunt, and I can see his point only too well. At tea after hunting he would let off steam by listing the people, and there were many, who would not be welcome with his private pack. I sometimes indulge in fantasy myself!

I do not remember many horse boxes at that time, they were few and far between; but they did have one at

Quenby for the far meets. The Quorn had just acquired a hound van, but it was seldom used.

When my horses were stabled at Gaddesby I used to hunt on Saturdays with the Quorn, as well as Mondays and Fridays. The Saturday meets were a long way off so Martin used to take my horse by train. This entailed being at Brooksby Station by 6.30 a.m. to box up, the train would leave at 7 a.m., going through Syston to Leicester – then out on another line to either Kegworth or Hathern where he would unbox at about 9 and ride on to the meet, for which he would be very early.

Martin reminds me that I always managed to miss the 5 o'clock train home, so that he had to ride, getting back to Gaddesby about the time the pub was shutting, 10 p.m.

I had an old heavy-weight horse I used to ride on Saturdays, called Buoyant. Lord Sefton had given him to Charlie Clarke because he pulled so, and Charlie gave him to me, presumably for the same reason. I found that if one accepted the fact that Buoyant only had two paces, galloping flat out, or standing still, he did not pull at all; but we used to go home very fast indeed if I was riding him! I only recall one contretemp with him, when Buoyant was convinced that we could get through a gate which was swinging shut, and I did not think it possible. Buoyant was perfectly right, but the gate slammed shut behind us, right in Harold Nutting's face, who was not particularly pleased.

On a Monday, if the meet was ten or twelve miles away, Martin would leave about 8.30 a.m. with my two horses, having first done them, plaited their manes and had his own breakfast. He would ride my second horse after the meet until we changed horses at about 2 p.m. when he rode my first horse home – most probably he would come out to meet me at the end of the day.

The second horsemen were obliged to assemble at the meet; no one was allowed to come out later. If a groom was seen on a road by himself he would get a rocket. Fred Lander, the huntsman's second horseman was in charge of all the others, and they had to obey him, and never go off on their own. It was all very strict. If hounds ran into the Belvoir or Cottesmore the second horses had to wait in Quorn country, it was forbidden to cross the border. On several occasions they failed to find us at all, and often they trotted for miles round the roads, probably doing more than our first horses had done.

Martin tells me that once, when the meet was about 8 miles away, and he knew hounds were coming back towards Gaddesby, he disobeyed the rules, brought my first horse to the meet and went back for the second. Riding up the road to Ashby Pastures later in the day to his horror he met hounds followed by the entire Field trotting towards him – Martin shot through a gate, hoping not to be seen, as luckily there was quite a thick fog – but Sir Harold spotted him and asked, 'Is Fred (Lander) down there?' 'Yes sir,' Martin replied untruthfully. 'Well get him' Harold shouted. When we had passed Martin hurried round to the other side of the Pastures, where fortunately he found Fred and the others and delivered his message.

George Barker who was huntsman of the Quorn from 1929 until '59 told me that he had to leave kennels at 4 a.m. for cubhunting at say Billesdon Coplow, if the meet was at 6.30. My mind boggles at the hour the hunt servants must have got up. In the season proper they would ride home from the far meets, arriving back at the kennels very late and in pitch dark.

But in some ways life was much easier for a huntsman then, though not for the lower ranks. There was a far larger staff in kennels and stables, which perhaps was due to the wages being infinitesimal compared to what they are today. I believe at one time George himself, as huntsman, got £16 a month.

Michael Farrin (our Quorn huntsman since 1968) tells me that in his first season hunting hounds, he was driving the hound van picking up flesh when he called at John Folwell's (George Barker's son-in-law). George, who lived next door, appeared in the yard and stopped in astonishment at seeing Michael. 'What – knacker-man as well?' he demanded in shocked tones. Michael explained that he was the only one available with a heavy goods driving licence. George shook his head, saying, 'When I was put on as huntsman, I was asked to hunt hounds four days a week and shoot the other two – and I did.'

In those days there was no vaccination against distemper, about 50 per cent of the puppies died of it, so many more young hounds were sent out to walk than are today. If distemper got into the kennel many of the old hounds would die as well. In 1930 George sent 53 couple of hound puppies out to walk, then in 1931 22½ couple were put on. I see that the late Duke of Gloucester walked puppies that year; and before that both he and the Prince of Wales (the late Duke of Windsor) had walked them. (An idea comes to my mind – but perhaps not!)

George fed his hounds on oatmeal puddings and meat which was always cooked. He and George Tongue who hunted the Belvoir were very famous in their hey day; and of course are still remembered by all the older fraternity.

Chatty Hilton-Green who was at the peak of his career as amateur huntsman had just taken the Cottesmore from James Baird, he hunted hounds, with Lord Sefton acting field master. Gordon Coleman, who lived at Scal-

ford, was Master of the Belvoir, Charles Tonge had been
Joint with him, but left in '31, but in 1934 he was joined
by Toby Greenall (now Lord Daresbury Master of the
Limerick). Toby did not dress as an MFH but acted as
field master in swallow tails and top hat, but there was
never any doubt who was master!

At Quenby there were often guests staying for the
weekend, sometimes rather grand ones; but there was
always the schoolroom where the boys and I could retire
if feeling ante social; or Harold's sitting room, where one
could read undisturbed while he telephoned his hunting
plans. Most of the visitors congregated in the big hall
where a huge log fire burned.

I do recall one incident when Enid Nutting took to
match-making, and decided that John ought to marry
Prim Rollo (Bill's daughter – who married David Niven
during the war.) John thought it an excellent idea, but
told his mother that he was too shy, and did not know
how to propose. Enid therefore wrote to John, who was
with his regiment, enclosing a letter for him to copy
proposing marriage to Prim. At the same time she wrote
to Prim inviting her to stay a weekend at Quenby, but
unfortunately she put the letters in the wrong envelopes!
The whole affair became a huge joke and wedding bells
were forgotten; John and Prim were both much too
young in any case.

At that period practical jokes were very much in vogue.
One spring Monica Sheriffe helped Enid plan a very
successful leg-pull on a lady who they thought was rather
keen on Harold. Procuring a straw bag for sending salmon in, and a printed label 'From Sir Harold Nutting,
Bart. Achentoul, Kinbrace' (his Scottish estate) they dis-
patched it to the lady in question, but instead of a salmon
it contained a bream which had been dead for a very long

time and was exceedingly high. I gather the recipient's affection for Harold waned very rapidly!

Many of the dances at Craven Lodge were fancy dress (I know I considered that a small moustache improved my looks enormously!). There were some very extraordinary outfits, and the parties usually became fairly wild. My favourite incident was when a very attractive lady insisted on swinging from the chandelier. This cabaret was not as popular as she had hoped, even her escort got bored and repaired to the bar for a drink. The result was that when she sank gracefully into his arms, as she thought, there was no one there so she fell to the floor, breaking her ankle.

4

MARRIAGE

When Tony and I were married he was in the Blues. The Regiment alternated between London and Windsor, so life was very civilised. We hunted in the winter, Tony played polo for his Regiment in the summer, and we went racing a good deal.

It seems funny now to think that in those days if we went out in London to any restaurant or night club, not only was everyone in evening dress, but Tony was obliged to wear a white tie and tails.

Tony's grandmother had lost her memory, and she lived in the big house at Gumley with two nurses to look after her. We kept our horses in the stables at Gumley, but took various small houses to hunt from.

As well as the Quorn and Belvoir we hunted with the Fernie, which was a good country with large enclosures and big fences. Bert Peaker had hunted hounds for some years, and Sir Julian Cahn, who lived at Stamford, near Loughborough, was Master of the Fernie in '37 for two years. He was rather an eccentric MFH and I think that the meet was the only part of a days hunting which he really enjoyed. He would only stay out for an hour or so and then retire into the back of his Rolls Royce, where he would find a three-course lunch ready for him, including an orange souffle, which apparently was his favourite dish.

Out hunting Sir Julian Cahn had riding with him a man carrying an axe, ready to demolish any obstacle in his master's way; but if the worst came to the worst and there was a ditch, the master would dismount, the groom would jump the horse over, and then Sir Julian would remount.

Jacko Allerton (Lord Allerton who lived at Loddington) was field master. One day when by 11.45 there was still no sign of the master, who quite often did not turn up at all, Jacko told Peaker to move off. At 12 o'clock Sir Julian arrived with two business friends who he hoped to impress as master of a famous pack of hounds. But of course, as we were by then drawing Bunkers Hill, there was not a soul left at the meet. Sir Julian Cahn lost his temper and storming with rage caught us up at Laughton Hills. Brushing Jacko away, as he tried to explain why we had not waited, the master proceeded to be extremely abusive to the huntsman in front of the entire Field. As Peaker had only obeyed orders in moving off when told to, this struck us as most unfair, so Tony rode up to Sir Julian Cahn saying, 'If you must behave like that, don't do it on my land – go somewhere else.' Then Tony and I and Audrey Bellville, (a great friend of our's who lived at Kibworth, and is now Audrey Bouverie) and a few more turned and rode home in disgust.

That evening a huge black Rolls Royce drew up at the house at Loddington where we were living, and a very smart chauffeur delivered an envelope addressed to Tony containing an apology from Sir Julian Cahn and a cheque for one thousand pounds. Unfortunately the

Opening meet of the Quorn Hunt, 1954. Left to right the author with Mr D Aldridge (secretary) and Colonel G A Murray Smith (MFH)

Three Quorn huntsmen. Jack Littleworth (left), George Barker (centre) with newly engaged Michael Farrin, in his first season (1968)

Coming out of kennels. Unique picture of
Quorn hounds and huntsman Michael Farrin

cheque was made out to the Fernie Hunt and not to Tony.

Soon after we were married we took a small house in Guilsborough for a few months, still keeping our horses at Gumley and hunting in Leicestershire, but we did have a few days with the Pytchley, which we found rather wired even in those days. I remarked to Tony how smartly turned out the Pytchley Field was, but all he said was, 'What a pity they don't spend more on their country and less on their clothes', which I thought a fair comment.

One season Tony was delighted, he had three months leave; but when he told Sam Ashton this, Sam looked surprised, saying, 'Only three months? I never took less than nine.'

At a moments notice, because all our horses were exhausted or lame, and we seemed to have nothing to ride, we went to ski in Austria. It was the greatest fun, so we planned to do the same the following year. This turned out to be a flop, as it had just thawed in England after some hard weather, while out there it had not snowed enough for the ski-ing to be any good. Donnie Player, who had come with us, Tony and I sat reading the hunting accounts in *The Times* with envy for three days, and then could bear it no longer and hurried home.

Tony had a very good black charger which we both used to hunt; Tony incurred the grave displeasure of the War Office because I rode him in a point to point and lamed him. He also had a charming horse suitably named Crikey, which always bucked when one got on. After winning the regimental cross country race Crikey bucked Tony off when he tried to remount him to hunt afterwards. He owned another horse which always neighed loudly when he jumped a big fence, whether with pride, joy, or horror I don't know! but Admiral Beatty called him 'the musical horse'.

We were once asked to stay at Castle Ashby by Lord Northampton for Tony to shoot, and were aghast to receive a letter inquiring if our valet and ladies maid would be coming with us by car, or separately by train. We took Tony's soldier servant, but said that my maid was ill, as in fact she did not exist.

5

THE WAR

The 1939-40 season was the greatest fun, nothing much was happening in the war, my husband and his regiment were stationed at Southwell, where we took a house until February when they went to Palestine.

The hunting was marvellous with very few people out, and sport was as good as ever. The Field would consist of some officers in uniform and a few locals; there was a wonderful pack of hounds (The Quorn who else?) and still all that glorious grass. Of course we realised how lucky we were to be able to hunt at all, and that we must make the most of it; it might be a long time before we hunted again.

One lady who had hunted in Leicestershire for years and had married three times, without ever having to change her initials, was so upset at the thought of her third husband, who was in the Foot Guards, having to go to the war, that to prevent him going she shot him in the bottom with a 12 bore gun as he was climbing over a fence out shooting.

When Tony went to Palestine he took as his charger a very beautiful horse of his own, St Anthony, who had been bred by Jack Bellville at Kibworth. He rode him all the time until the regiment was mechanised in 1940 when he gave him to Bruce Hobbs, who was out there in a Yeomanry Regiment. The horse later broke his leg in the Jebel Druz and had to be put down.

Martin had joined the Blues at the outbreak of war, and went with Tony as his groom, becoming his soldier servant when they gave up their horses.

Sir Harold Nutting retired as Master of the Quorn in 1940, but continued to take a great interest in the hounds, and was chairman for many years.

Anthony Nutting told me that when he escaped from France just before Dunkirk, the first thing he did on arrival in this country was to telephone to his father. From Quenby he was informed that Sir Harold was staying at Badminton. When Anthony finally contacted him to explain how he had managed to get out of France, and what a terrible disaster it all was, he then asked his father what he was doing in Gloucestershire. 'What do you think I am doing at Badminton at this time of year?' Harold asked quite testily, 'judging Master's young entry of course!'

I managed with some ingenuity, to get to Palestine in the spring of 1940. Ruth Wood (now Lady Halifax) and I shared a small house in Nathanya, where our husbands used to come whenever they could, and we would all have terrific picnics on the beaches. When Tony and Charles could get a few days off we would go to Jerusalem, Syria or Trans Jordan. We stayed with a sheik in the desert, and we went to some camel races at Beersheba which were fascinating. No starting stalls, but the camels had to be in a recumbent position when the flag fell; and it took a great deal of time and some very bad language (Arabic) to persuade them to lie down, then even more abuse to get them up again at the 'off'. I would hazard a guess that the camels did not enjoy racing, judging by their vitriolic expression and continuous grunts and groans.

The remounts were in Nathanya, and in charge of them were John Smith-Maxwell and Leslie Jones, both of whom afterwards became military policemen. (Poachers become game-keepers I remember they said!)

We used to have a wonderful time trying out all the remount horses, usually along the vast stretches of sand on the beaches; and there were some very high class horses among them. On one occasion we staged a tremendous betting coup at the nearby races. John had found the most superb race horse in his remounts; he was called Sultan and had been in training in England. John entered him for the ladies' race, but the plan was kept a complete secret. No one was told, or shown the horse, which we practiced jumping off, and trained in private on the sands. In fact, when we arrived at the races John and Leslie almost overdid it, saying 'Just a nag from our remounts, we entered because Ulrica was so disappointed she had nothing to ride.' Sultan only appeared, looking magnificent, at the last moment when the bets were on. There were about twelve in the race, mostly arabs. Sultan duly won by 8 lengths at 8-1, and John, Leslie and Tony cleaned up, while most of our friends were simply furious that they had not been told. My only flat race, which makes a nice average!

In the evenings we would reminisce about the hunting we had had, and the horses we had ridden. John and Leslie used to mix a lethal cocktail in a small milk churn, which as far as I could see consisted of a bottle of brandy and one of gin, with just a dash of fruit juice; anyway it was delicious.

John had been Master of Horse to Sir Keith and Lady

Nuttall, who had lived in Cheshire, before they bought Lowesby and moved to Leicestershire. The job entailed buying the hunters, schooling them, arranging who rode which, running the whole outfit and of course hunting every day. Leslie Jones had done the same for Mrs Murray-Graham who was James Hanbury's mother. I recall how we all agreed (over the milk churn) that there would be no more jobs like that after the war – how right we were.

Tony and his brother officers in the Household Cavalry Regiment were at Tulkarm; also in Palestine were the Wiltshire Yeomanry, in which my eldest brother was serving, the Sherwood Rangers and various other regiments including the Greys. The war in Europe was static, so we had the most enjoyable summer. In the autumn we were told that wives had to leave Palestine, though very few had succeeded in getting out there at all. Four of us went to India, Ruth, Primrose Cadogan, Mary Roxburgh and me, with the hope that we might be able to return from there.

Our first weekend in India was spent in Simla with the Viceroy, Lord Linlithgow, and his family. Here I had my first and only sight of Mr Ghandi arriving in a rickshaw to see the Viceroy.

Primrose Cadogan and I went down to Bombay, where we stayed in Ali Khan's house. (Primrose was his sister-in-law). But soon after I arrived in Bombay I met Neville and Dina Wadia, (she was Mr Jinnah's daughter). Mr Jinnah was head of the Muslim League and when India and Pakistan separated he was Governor-General of the latter. Dina was small and incredibly beautiful – we met at a drinks party in aid of War Charities. Dina asked me to stay for a weekend, which surprised everyone as she was extremely anti-British at the time. Anyhow I duly went for the weekend, and stayed for a year! – doing various war effort jobs. Tony managed to come and visit me when he was on sick leave; having been ill after a strenuous summer fighting wars in Iraq, Syria and Iran.

In Palestine Tony had hunted with Col 'Mouse' Townsend and the Ramle Vale Hunt; where he said they had had quite a lot of trouble with the Arab farmers, who for some reason did not like them riding over their wheat! He also told me that when the first convoy came through from Bagdad to Haifa, peering over the tail board of the last lorry were two fox hounds; a draft from the Royal Bagdad Foxhounds to the Ramle Vale.

Leicestershire seemed a far cry, but what a joy it was to find myself out with the Bombay Jackal Club. Starting off in the dark just before dawn, a jackal was always found so quickly that I suspect it must have been a 'bagged one'; but hounds would hunt it at great speed over the tiny paddy (rice) fields surrounded by banks which we would jump, often ending by running up a mountain. The going was rock hard, but what fun it was to ride and to hear hounds again.

On one occasion I followed the huntsman when he swam a very wide deep river on his horse. It was the most alarming experience as I had no idea a horse swam so deep. Soon I could only see my mount's ears and nostrils, and was up to my shoulders in the water. When we emerged on the other side hounds turned sharp right and there were the other followers who had crossed safely by a bridge. This I must admit was most annoying. (And what a dark stain I made on the snow white upholstery of the Government House car!)

I also spent some time with the Lumleys in Bombay and Poona. Roger Lumley, (the late Lord Scarborough) was Governor of Bombay at the time. It was at Poona that

I was able to fulfil my ambition to drive a four-in-hand. I think one of my proudest moments was when I drove the team to the races. We arrived at a spanking trot, all the police waving us on as it was the Government House carriage, to find an extremely sharp turn to the right through a very narrow gateway. The Syce spoke no English, so could give no advice, and I realised that we were going much too fast; but I remembered my father telling me that as the leaders turned you pulled the wheelers the other way. Anyhow we thundered through at breakneck speed, and to my delight, not to mention astonishment, we did not hit the gate.

I returned to England for a while in 1942, by sea round the Cape, the ship zig-zagging to avoid the Japanese, who had just come into the war.

The OC Troops had DTs and used to behave in a very peculiar manner. One evening I went to have a drink with him and found two trays with twenty-four large cocktails. 'Oh, it's a party', I said. 'No, only you and me,' he replied, 'but it's such a bore ringing for the steward'.

We docked at Glasgow, where I succeeded in catching the night train down to London, sitting squeezed between a large Naval officer who slept on my shoulder all the way, and two Air Force types. As all travel was secret in those days, I had been unable to let anyone know when I was leaving, let alone arriving home, so no one was expecting me. I rang my parents in London, and reached their Sussex home at Findon, more dead than alive, about 10 a.m. longing only for bed. However it was broken to me that the Crawley and Horsham were meeting at the house that very morning. Perking up instantly I asked if there was a horse for me which there was, so hastily finding something to wear, out I went. What a perfect homecoming, and wonderful to find in the middle of a world war that foxhunting somehow kept going.

I returned to India again a year later, to do cyphers for SOE. Travelling in war time was not the height of comfort. This time I was one of four civilians on a troop ship in the first convoy to go through the Mediterranean when it was re-opened. It was very over-crowded, and 'Dry'! We never moved without our life jackets and our 'panic bags'. (These were necessities in case we took to the life boats – my 'panic bag' was full of nylons and lip sticks, and a bottle of brandy which I had already drunk.) I shared a cabin with two Wrens and a nurse, we were supposed to sleep fully dressed, but I never did.

Arriving in India I quickly extricated myself from a two-year contract in Meerut, and went to New Delhi which was far more interesting, and I spent two fascinating years working there.

When I heard Tony might be getting back to England, with a little influence from Viceroy's House I got on to an aeroplane home. It was a 'stripped' Liberator, terribly noisy and we sat on the floor. I remember vividly there were two German prisoners (U-Boat captains) on the plane; and as they were blindfolded they fell flat on their faces every single time they got in or out of the plane. We spent four nights enroute, but luckily no super VIP appeared to push me off, and we returned safely to England.

After 1940 I never went to Leicestershire until after the war. It must have been very difficult to keep a pack of hounds going at all during that period.

With the Quorn, when Harold Nutting gave up, Phillip Cantrell-Hubberstay acted Master for the committee until '47 when he fell dead from his horse out hunting. Fred Mee, a big farmer in Shepshed, proved invaluable to the Quorn, providing food for horses and hounds, (he was to be Joint Master from '48 to '51, although he had given up riding to hounds by then).

George Barker, the Huntsman, must have worked wonders during that time to cope with getting about the country, and feeding the hounds, apart from trying to hunt the fox. I am told that he grew cabbages and potatoes behind the kennels, which he boiled to feed hounds. In 1939 (before the war broke out) $36\frac{1}{2}$ couple were sent out to walk, then in '40 $11\frac{1}{2}$ and in '41 only $8\frac{1}{2}$.

Toby Daresbury was still Master of the Belvoir, and operated from Hyde Park Barracks, with George Tongue running the kennels and hunting hounds. Toby left the Belvoir in '47 to take the Limerick, where he hunted hounds for 25 years and is still Joint Master. James Hanbury took the Belvoir in '47.

Boodley Hilton-Green looked after the Cottesmore, with Herbert Norman hunting hounds. Much later when she was Lady Daresbury, Boodley was killed out hunting with the Limerick. She was one of the best riders across country I have ever seen, and was completely fearless.

6

HUNTING AFTER
THE WAR

After the war as Gumley, (which has now been pulled down) was still requisitioned by the army, and the Rectory, which Tony had bought, was not ready, we took Whissenthorpe from Leo Partridge. I cannot describe the discomfort, the house was bitterly cold, and nothing worked very well, if at all! The electricity (we made our own) was so feeble that the lamps only showed a dim glow when switched on. When we grumbled to Leo about it, his only comment was that there was enough light to drink and to talk, and what more did we need to do in the evenings?

It was a particularly cold winter; when we could hunt that was fine, but it was not much fun being snowed up at Whissenthorpe.

Luckily after one season we were able to move back to the Rectory at Gumley. A permit was necessary for any alterations, and the only way to have a second bathroom put in was to have an old-fashioned bath moved up from the big house.

Clothes coupons were still needed to get any form of clothing, and petrol was rationed. The great thing was to get farm petrol, (a different colour) for cattle trucks and travel everywhere in them, with or without horses. I recall Tim Llewellen-Palmer coming to dine at Gumley from Hoby, about 20 miles, on his tractor.

We hunted with the Fernie, the Quorn and the Belvoir. It was rather a different picture than before the war. No one had second horses, and the turn out had certainly deteriorated; there were fewer people out, and of course with no petrol, practically no car followers. Although there was now quite a bit of plough, and some wire had gone up, it was the most tremendous fun to be hunting again. Hunters were difficult to find, and those sent over from Ireland were terribly green by old standards.

Tony was lucky to buy a super black horse from the Nuttings, which had been bred to win chases for their sons. He was six years old and unbroken, by My Prince out of a Cottage mare and was called The Emir.

John Smith-Maxwell used to get some useful horses from Ireland, and as we were great friends of his, we had first pick. We used to stay at Moreton-in-the-Marsh with John, his wife Joan, and family, and they often came up to us at Gumley.

John, beside dealing a bit and judging hunters, also wrote very entertaining hunting articles, and reported on shows. He told me that not only did many owners ask him to give their horse a good write up, but on one occasion a hunter judge suggested to him that it would be nice if he would say what a particularly good rider and judge she was!

About this time although he was still in the army Tony had an inclination to take a pack of hounds in Ireland; so we went over there to have a look, and stayed with his uncle, Tommy Ainsworth. The first day hunting with the

United my hireling fell jumping into a sunken road, broke his leg and ribs and died within minutes. As he had fallen on my leg, my ankle was smashed into small pieces, and I retired to a nursing home in Cork. (Distinctly put off hunting in Ireland).

The nuns were very kind; I was looked after by one who I think was called Sister Angostura, or it sounded like that! She arrived on the scene every morning at 7 a.m. having already prayed in the chapel for over two hours. She remained on duty until 10 p.m. and never appeared to go off for any meals. She had one hour off, which she much looked forward to, on Sunday after-noons to take a walk.

Good as the nursing was, no one was able to set my ankle which needed a tricky operation, so Tony arranged for us to fly back to London, where it was successfully put together by Sir Reginald Watson-Jones.

A few years after the war had ended Leicestershire began to get back to normal. The outsiders re-appeared in the hunting field; some were newcomers and others had hunted pre-war; but they no longer took houses and became part of the country as in the old days, but now would come for the day.

A few people stayed the night before hunting at the Bell Hotel, Melton. These included the late Lord Ash-combe, the Myddeltons, and Rupert Watson, (now Lord Manton, who has hunted with us ever since, now living in Yorkshire.)

Sir George and Lady Earle had moved to Baggrave Hall from Thorpe Satchville, where they had lived since just before the war. They were both very well turned-out with hounds, she side saddle. George was always cour-teous to everyone, and went out of his way to be charm-ing to any strangers – Marjorie was the exact opposite;

she suffered from diabetes, and perhaps this made her behaviour so peculiar at times.

It was the most alarming experience to meet Marjorie Earle when she was driving her horse box, as she drove very fast in the middle of the road, and was quite liable to have a black out. Fred Earp once found her slumped over the driving wheel (the box luckily having stopped), and had to force sugar, which she always carried in her pocket, through her clenched teeth.

Marjorie was absolutely mad on hunting, and thought of nothing else. I remember when a very unpopular man, who had behaved extremely badly on various occasions was under discussion, Marjorie saying firmly, 'He can't be bad, he goes so well out hunting,' which was apparently her only criterion.

The pessimists who had said that hunting in the Shires was finished were proved wrong; though of course the days of all grass were gone for ever, and many new problems had cropped up.

I suppose scent was better in the old days, as pre-war grass was easier to hunt over than plough and crops. There would have been foiled grounds from cattle and sheep, but not all the fertilisers and sprays which are used today.

What conditions are required for scent to be good has been argued and written about ad infinitum; but it does seem to be obvious that some foxes smell more than others. This after all applies to people too!

George Barker told me that there was never a scent if one's hunting tie made one's neck sore. When I imparted this gem of knowledge to Teddy Bouskell-Wade he said, 'Then I simply must stop having my tie starched or we shall never have a scent.'

Teddy told me that on his first appearance with the

Quorn hounds after the war Phillip Cantrell-Hubbersty
rode up and asked him where he had been and why he
had not been out hunting. Teddy replied that he had
been abroad fighting the war. All Phillip said was, 'Well,
you will find subscriptions have gone up', and rode away.

In 1947 the Quorn had hard pad in kennels and lost
many hounds with it. It must have been heart-breaking
to see so many good hounds die, as there was apparently
nothing anyone could do to save them.

We saw a great deal of Arthur and Elizabeth Pilking-
ton, she was the eldest Harrison daughter, and they
hunted from Little Belvoir. We had many parties
together, and also used to stay with them in Yorkshire for
Doncaster races.

Liz later married Tony Burke and they went to live in
Ireland, where he was killed out hunting. Liz was Joint
Master of the Meath for some years, and now runs the
Stackallen Stud.

After the war the Army had provided us with a space-
ous flat in Hyde Park Barracks, looking over the Park. I
remember the week we moved in Tony had to rush over
to Ireland as his Mother was ill. He left me with a key to
the small door into barracks from Knightsbridge, as the
big gate was always locked at night. Returning quite late
from rather a smart dinner party, I was dropped off at
the little door, which I opened with my key. I could not
find the light but felt sure that I should be able to find my
way, so said goodnight, shut the door, and set off down
the passage. The going became rather rough, and I
seemed to be going up hill – when suddenly the lights
were switched on, and I found myself half way up a heap
of coal; eyed in astonishment by three immense troopers.
Summoning all the dignity I could in the circumstances I
said 'It is alright – I live here.' To which one of them

replied 'I know you do, but you are not going the right way.' They then escorted me to the flat.

When I recounted the experience to Tony on his return, all he said was 'Very lucky they did know who you were.'

Photo: Frank H. Meads

Michael Farrin on The Harbourer with
Tony Wright and the bitch pack

Quorn Hunt. HRH Prince Charles waiting
outside Prince of Wales Covert

7

SPANISH
HOLIDAYS

Soon after the war ended Tony and I visited Spain, which we both adored, and made many friends in Madrid and Andalucia. We went there whenever we could get away each summer.

One year Margot Larios, who was then married to Miguel (the late Duke of Primo de Rivera, later Spanish Ambassador to London) arranged a splendid riding tour for us. We had discussed the idea often when staying with her at Berlanguilla, (a farm house near Jerez de la Frontera). The plan was to ride from Jerez to Algeciras, through the Sierra, spending one night en route.

All was arranged and Tony and I flew from London, staying in Madrid on our way. The first person we met in Madrid was Margot's brother, Pepito (Duke of Lerma) who we told of our forthcoming adventure. (Having no idea that it was a secret!). Miguel was living in Madrid, so Pepito apparently hastened to tell him all about it, and the fact that we were all going to ride Miguel's horses, which made him absolutely furious.

Hardly had we greeted Margot in Jerez when she received a telegram from Miguel advising her of his extreme displeasure and his imminent arrival by night train at Jerez on the actual morning of our departure.

We were all in some trepidation when he appeared, knowing that he had every intention of stopping us. He said politely, 'Hullo Ulrica, how lovely to see you', then pushed Margot into a raspberry bush. However, he quickly regained his temper, and on seeing the preparations for the trip, changed his mind, and adding two enormous flasks of brandy to our luggage, decided to come with us.

There were seven of us, Miguel, Margot, her sister Marilu, Tony and I, and a groom carrying all our things. With us also was a mounted Civil Guard, to protect us from bandits, as the country was extremely wild, and we were quite likely to get lost in the mountains.

On the first day we stopped to light a fire of charcoal, on which Margot cooked a delicious paella; then the night was spent in a tiny hacienda (pub) in a small village. We arrived in Algeciras very late the next evening. Most of the ride was taken at a slow and stately walk, but occasionally when we had had a swig of Miguel's brandy we would gallop for a short distance.

I remember as we meandered through the mountains Miguel telling me of his imprisonment by the Reds in the Civil War. His brother Jose Antonio was in the same prison, and Miguel had been allowed to see him once to say goodbye before he was shot. I asked if it was not desperately dull to be kept in solitary confinement for over a year, but he explained that it was not dull at all, because every day he thought that they would take him out and shoot him.

I may say that Tony, who was the only one of the party who had been riding, (down the Mall on and off guard at Whitehall) was the only person to get a sore knee.

It was on one of our visits to Spain that we first met the Duke of Albuquerque, and in the most dramatic fashion. Since then I have admired tremendously Beltran Albuquerque who has ridden and won races all over Europe. For several years (until he was stopped by the race course doctors) he rode in the Grand National, when he was a rather more advanced age than most steeplechase jockeys, and with his broken bones pinned together with screws and plates. To return to our first encounter – Tony, David Westmorland, Rowland St Oswald and I were driving back to San Sebastian after an excellent dinner out in the country, when we inadvertently hit a tree very hard indeed, which completely incapacitated the car. Sitting disconsolately by the road side miles from nowhere, wondering what to do, a passing car pulled up driven by Beltran Albuquerque. Rowland luckily speaks fluent Spanish, as Beltran's English was non-existent, and explained our predicament. Beltran said he was happy to take us back to San Sebastian, but that first we should have to accompany him to a party. So we all spent most of the night at a very smart party, for which we were not at all suitably dressed; but it turned out to be a super party, with flamenco, and then we were duly driven back in the early hours – this time avoiding all trees.

We used to stay with Beltran and Anne Domecq for the Jerez Fair; a typical Spanish festival where everyone rides and drives beautifully decorated horses, and no one ever seems to go to bed, and sherry comes out of one's ears by the end of it all.

To see eight horses as a team pulling a carriage, (three abreast, then three, then two) is most impressive, especially when driven at speed round a small enclosure. The liveries worn by the coachmen and the fabulous harness has to be seen to be believed. But I did make a very tactless remark when I mentioned the Andalusian horses 'dishing' which I was curtly told that they were meant to do!

8

TONY
IS MASTER

Tony became Master of the Quorn in 1954. It was not a particularly opportune moment for him, because that year he was not only High Sheriff of Leicestershire but he had also just been made Colonel of the Leicestershire Yeomanry.

So he had a lot on his plate already when Harold Nutting, Quorn Chairman, rang him up and asked him to take the Quorn hounds in place of Ronnie Strutt (Lord Belper) who had resigned.

Living at Gumley had its complications – some of the Quorn meets were a long way off, as were the farmers' suppers and other activities, and it took a lot of time to visit round the country. We kept our horses at the kennels at Barrow-on-Soar, and Martin moved over there to be our Stud Groom. But we seemed to spend a great deal of time on the road.

I had just become very keen on show jumping, at which I never had a startling success. I remember when being presented with a rosette (probably equal third or such like accolade) the Lady Mayoress told me how nice it was to see some one ride round looking as if they were out hunting. I was disappointed as I had rather hoped that I looked as if I was show jumping!

George Barker was very disapproving and thought that the right people in other words foxhunters, simply did not mix with show jumpers.

It was great fun, and gave me a wonderful excuse to jump fences all the summer. I used to enjoy enormously going over to Jack Talbot-Ponsonby, Ted Williams or Robin Leyland for a school. Jack Ponsonby had a paddock full of jumps of all descriptions at Welford, but they were so beautifully built, with the distance between each fence measured so accurately that it was almost impossible to hit anything. The result what that I would go off to the next show convinced that I was bound to win – only to be disillusioned.

I think that I enjoyed the schooling part much more than the actual shows, (except perhaps the rare occasions when I won something), but I found the waiting about very tedious.

I had one wonderful horse whom I bought from Ted Williams. Lively Lord was very beautiful, very intelligent, and was a magnificent jumper. We had great fun together hunting, hunter trialing, and competing in shows.

If Tony had bought a new hunt horse, I would look over the stable door and think out loud, 'I wonder if he would show jump?', and Martin would say, 'I don't know – but I am sure he will have to try.'

When Tony took the Quorn it was the first time we had hunted in the Tuesday Country, which is quite a different experience, being very wild with rocks and bracken and stone walls; but splendid to hunt in. One of my favourite parts of the country is still around the Monastery. I remember a superb hunt from Lea Wood right across the forest to ground on Sharpley. It would not be possible now, as the M1 cuts the country in half.

I do not think people realise what a tremendous number of duties there are for an MFH besides arranging the days hunting and then swanning about in a hunting cap in front of a large field. There are endless suppers, skittle evenings, pony club events, puppy shows, and the more you can get involved in the country the better. If possible it is of the greatest advantage for the master to attend the agricultural show, a hunt cricket match, or gymkhana, any NFU activity, and the local harvest festival supper (if invited). Of course it is all time-consuming, not to mention the petrol, especially if you are not living in the country.

A new master must try to visit as many farmers as possible. The people he has not seen will be quick to broadcast the fact. When you do call you may be kept standing in the rain, or perhaps you will be asked in and plied with tea or whisky, which I always find is, in either case, far stronger than what I am accustomed to.

I recall Tony having a very tricky visit early in his career as master, when his Staffordshire bull terrier killed the house cat before the very eyes of the rather awkward lady he had come to see.

An MFH is expected automatically to be a good judge of both horse and hound, and to be ready and willing to accept invitations to judge either, even though he may be an indifferent horseman, and have never taken the slightest interest in hounds (except perhaps to ride on them).

John Smith-Maxwell gave me many useful hints when I first judged a hunter class. The most important point, he explained, was to read the schedule carefully, so that you knew exactly what you had to judge. For example with a pony class – was it the best pony under 13.2 ridden by a child, or the best pony suitable to be ridden by a child. John told me that on one occasion his car had broken down, so that he only arrived at the show just as his class, which he was under the impression was 'small hunter', was entering the ring. When he was riding them and came to the animal he had pulled in about sixth, as he dismounted after riding it, he said to the exhibitor, 'A lovely ride, but really more of a hack than a small hunter.' The man looking surprised said, 'But this is the hack class.' John, never at a loss, replied, 'My dear chap, go to the top of the class then.'

The first time Tony and I judged together at a very small show just after the war, Martin told us afterwards that he had had the car handy with the engine running in case we made a nonsense of it. It showed a certain lack of confidence in our judgement I thought!

James Hanbury told me that the first time he had to judge at a puppy show he arranged a complicated series of signals with his huntsman, George Tongue, who sat in a strategic position at the ringside, where he could sign to James how to place the young hounds. It all worked splendidly until his co-judge asked James why he did not like a certain dog, which of course totally stumped him.

While he was still Master of the Quorn, about 22 or 23 years ago, Tony bought the house at Gaddesby, where I have lived ever since. It needed a great deal doing to it, as it had no electric light, and was a bit derelict. One very great advantage it now has, is that the garden is a certain find, as foxes live undisturbed in the well preserved brambles.

When Denis Aldridge, who had always been tremendously popular with the farmers, retired as Secretary of the Quorn, Jonathon Inglesant took over from him to be secretary for the next eighteen years.

Jonathon is a real countryman, and hated being away from Leicestershire even for a day. He did the work of about three men, and was unflappable in a crisis, and never seemed to get cross or lose his temper. He had a great sense of humour so it was always fun going round with him, and everyone was pleased to see him.

In '58 the Belvoir had a new Master. John King, (Sir John since the new year honours of '79) came from the Badsworth to join James Hanbury and Lord Belper; and certainly did a great deal for the Belvoir in his fourteen years of mastership, and is their chairman now. John lives in our country, as he bought Friars Well, Wartnaby, which had been built by Donnie and Leila Player. He owns quite a lot of land there, and I must say I wish that he had more grass and less plough. But on the other hand he does have plenty of foxes on his estate, and we can go when and where we like, which is more than can be said of Kingston, Lord Belper's home, which is also in Quorn country, but where we are not at all welcome.

Also in '58 Bob Hoare became Master of the Cottesmore and hunted hounds. He had more enthusiasm than anyone I have ever known. He was always prepared to come and judge absolutely anything, from horses and hounds, to horn blowing, dairy maids or ankles! Join any party that was going on, or stand up and make a speech at a moment's notice; and what is more he always appeared to be enjoying himself immensely, and I think he was.

At the Royal Show one year they had seven packs of hounds in the ring at the same time, so of course there was great confusion, and many of the huntsmen had more hounds than they had started with; but Bob was seen galloping round the ring with only one hound at his heels. Raymond Brooks-Ward gave out on the loud speaker, 'And now a cheer for Major Hoare and his one faithful hound.'

In '56 Lance Newton started the Melton Hunt Club, which has proved such an outstanding success, and helps the three Melton Hunts financially, runs a cross country race alternately in Quorn, Cottesmore and Belvoir country, and has one of the most important point to points of the year at Garthorpe.

Since Lance's death his wife Urkie has run the club most efficiently. Urkie and her family all hunt incessantly, and own land in Belvoir, Quorn and Cottesmore country.

9

HORSES

To enjoy hunting it is absolutely essential to be well mounted. A friend of mine married for a horse; a very sensible thing to do. Her most ardent suitor had mounted her on his superlative hunter for one whole season, at the end of which he suggested that it was time that she made up her mind whether she would marry him or not. She realised that if she said 'no' she could hardly expect him to produce her favourite animal for her any more; so it had to be 'yes'. Unfortunately, the horse broke down and never hunted again – but the marriage was a great success. Well I suppose it is as good a reason for getting married as any other.

I advocated in *Horse and Hound* buying horses from reputable dealers, rather than from friends, as this is apt to end beautiful friendships. The next week I met Simon Clarke, then Master of the Cottesmore, from whom I had bought a hunt horse that autumn. Simon said to me quite huffily, 'I thought that horse was a success – or did you never consider we were friends?'

I have always liked big horses, especially with the rough people there are around today. In fact I consider a big good one is better than a good little one.

The best horse I ever rode was Cottage Point who originally belonged to James Hanbury. Sold at auction he had a short and very unsuccessful sojourn in the Heythrop country. (Possibly like me he fancied Leicestershire!) John Smith-Maxwell, who was living at Moreton-in-the Marsh, rang us up to tell us that the new owners wanted to get rid of Cottage Point at any price; so Tony bought him, (through John) for less than half what he had fetched at auction.

The first time I rode Cottage, I was waiting while some one jumped a post and rails, when to my surprise Cottage leaped about ten foot in the air, took two strides in the other direction and jumped a place I should never have considered negotiable. This is quite a horse, I thought, and quickly annexed him as mine.

He was the bravest horse I ever rode, with the biggest jump, he never put in a short stride, just stood off any distance. He never looked where he was landing (which was sometimes a pity!) but on to where he could jump the next fence. He had an absolute passion for jumping, and if he saw anyone else jump an obstacle he just took off, giving the most enormous leap in sympathy. This entailed keeping a sharp look out which way he was pointing or some unsuspecting chum would be either knocked off his horse or knocked over, which was not always tremendously popular. Cottage would not ever wait his turn, but luckily for me, when I said, 'WHOA Cottage', everyone seemed to get out of the way.

As a matter of fact it can be very advantageous to ride a horse that won't wait, but it is absolutely maddening if other people do!

Before the foreigners spoiled the market, I used to get horses from Ireland. Boodley Daresbury was a wonderful judge of a horse, and had many contacts round Limerick. She used to find good quality hunters which made a habit of flying the banks, and were therefore rather a dangerous ride in Ireland. She would buy them and ring up one of her many friends in England who would be quite prepared to buy a horse 'blind' if Boodley recommended it.

It was always tremendous fun staying at Clonshire with the Daresburys and going horse coping with Boodley, though I must admit I was not madly keen on being forced to ride her own young horses, prior to our expedition, and even before breakfast. I remember one morning having just returned from the most hazardous ride, Boodley said, 'Now we must ride the green ones.' In horror I asked, 'What on earth do you call the ones we have just ridden?' 'Oh, they have been backed a month', she explained, 'the next lot have only been ridden for ten days.'

On one occasion we met a stationary ass cart in a grass lane. It required all our combined powers of persuasion and intrepid horsemanship to induce our mounts to sidle past. When this was finally accomplished Boodley turned to me and said proudly, 'You see they are alright with traffic.'

In County Cork a charming man took us round to look at some likely animals. Boodley, I found, had told him that I was so poor that unless he could produce a very cheap, but naturally brilliant horse, I would not be able to afford to hunt at all. It was a sad story and brought tears to his eyes; but when we bid him goodbye, he told me how pleased he was to have met me as he had seen so many pictures of me and my husband in *Horse and Hound*. (Tony was Master of the Quorn at the time) I was very embarrassed, feeling that if by chance he had believed it all, he must have thought Tony extremely mean! Boodley was unrepentant, and thought it a perfectly natural thing to have said.

Some years later Migs Greenall and I were staying at Clonshire, and Boodley took us out for a really hilarious day buying horses. One of the first animals we saw was quite a nice grey, which we wished to try, but unfortunately although we had brought a saddle with us, no bridle could be found. Finally, we discovered a cart horse bridle, complete with blinkers, which was broken at the top and tied together with pink ribbon. But it had no reins and Boodley was quite cross when neither Migs nor I would consent to ride without any, despite the fact that Boodley offered to lead the grey with her hand on the bit. In the end some binder twine was produced in place of reins, so all was well. Boodley bought the horse and named him Binder Twine.

The next animal we saw was small and black; his owner insisted on trotting him very fast over cobble stones in the yard, and jumping him over a single strand of wire back and forth. There was nowhere else to try him, and it did not strike me as typical of the Quorn country, but I bought him. He was called Brandy; I added 'Soda' and after hunting and then jumping him for one year, I sold him at a nice profit as a jumper. George Hobbs jumped him internationally with great success.

We saw many horses that day, finishing up in the dark at some deserted stables, where a note had been left for us, thoughtfully placed with a torch, saying, 'The mare you want to see is in the second box on the left'.

We got her out and I trotted her up in the pitch dark yard, while Boodley and Migs looked at her in the wavering beam of light from the torch. Migs, I thought rather bravely, bought her on the telephone later that night, without any idea what she looked like. However she was sent over to Migs in England and turned out to be a success.

Latterly I have bought horses in England. Robin Leyland provided me with some very good ones; he was always very expansive about their faults. 'He is sure to buck you off,' he would say, or, 'You will never hold him, but he might do Michael', or, 'You won't like the look of her, but she does jump.'

Great Expectations, who I bought from Eric Wright, was very nappy, and nobody liked her except me, but I adored her; she was brilliant. Since she broke down she has bred two very nice foals for Frank Hewitt, who has her now.

Hobson's Choice came from George Rich, and I have in fact, ridden him on 270 days hunting during the last six seasons. He is a great character; never misses a day, never puts a foot wrong, and adores hunting.

Aquarius who was given to me by Peter Pritchard, (one of the nicest and most unexpected presents I have ever had) was the ideal stamp of hunter to my mind, size, scope, quality as well as ability. Later I bought The Harbourer which Michael rides, from Peter Pritchard and he is a super bright chestnut horse.

John Betteridge sold me a beautiful big horse which I think is a bit extra. But just when I had solved a slight breaks problem, and was delighted with him, we had a very nasty accident when his hind legs fell through a concealed and very deep drain at Prestwold. I have not been able to ride him since, so I hope when he has recovered next year, he will prove as brilliant as I think.

But I could go on about my horses forever!

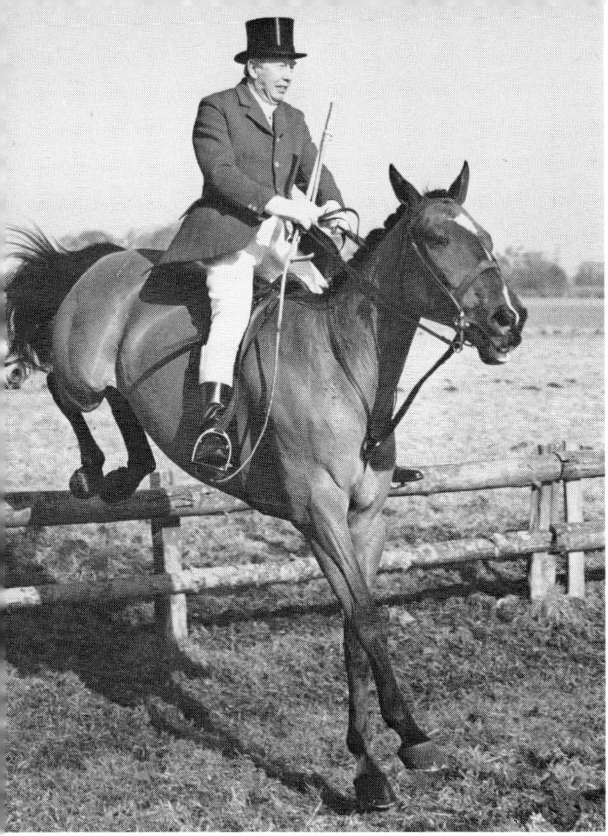

The Crown Equerry
Sir John Miller

Photo: Jim Meads

The author riding
Hobson's Choice,
on whom she has had
270 days' hunting

Photo: Jim Meads

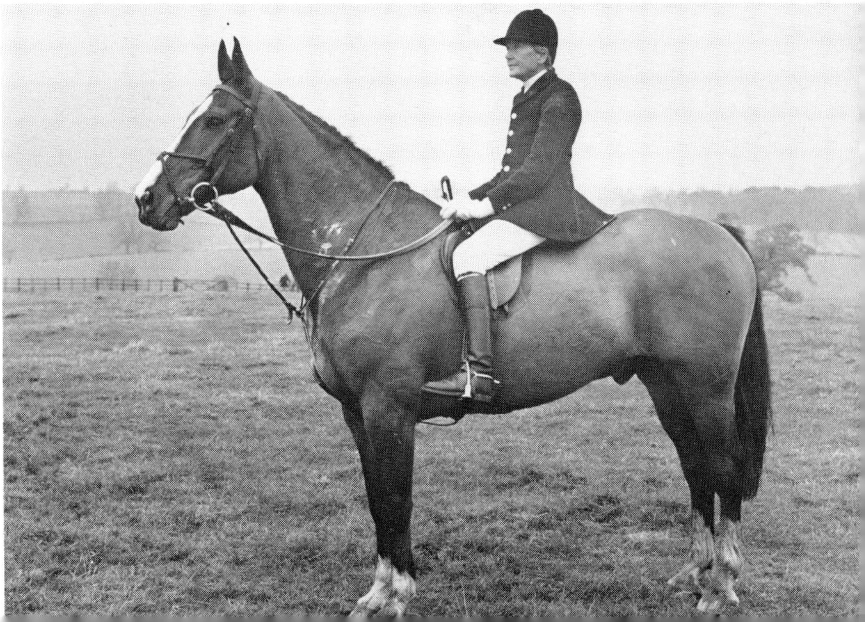

Quorn Hunt. The three joint-masters on a snowy day at Lowesby, Leicestershire
Captain Fred Barker, Mrs Ulrica Murray Smith and Mr James Teacher

Photo: Jim Meads

10

COPERS

George Rich and Dr Tom Connors both sell hunters in
the Quorn country, and would-be buyers come from far
and wide to see their horses. George and Barbara Rich
have a house and large riding school at Thorpe Satchville; Tom and Jill Connors live at Upper Broughton,
(not a bad place to live). Tom owns some very delectable
land on Muxlow Hill, all grass with very inviting fences
(which brings out the very worst in the Quorn Field!)

Tom, whose surgery is over as soon as possible on a
hunting morning, enjoys riding a hunt as much as anyone; but he is most unselfish in the way he will stop to
attend to anyone who has had a bad fall. (No matter from
whom they have bought their horse!) He always carries
morphia, which is in great demand with the fallen,
although one young lady did refuse it, having broken her
collar bone, saying that Tom's smile was enough!

Some years ago I was having lunch with the Riches,
when they lived at New Ingarsby, and found everyone in
a terrible flap. It appeared that a possible buyer had
come, by appointment, that morning to see a
heavyweight hunter. George had not had anything suit-

able in his yard, so, not wanting to put a new client off, he had rung Tom Connors to see if he could produce anything. Tom had promised to send a likely sort of horse over in the morning, but he wanted it back, if not sold, by the afternoon as he had someone coming to have a look.

George's troubles began when the client arrived before the horse, and refused to be fobbed off with drinks. On the spur of the moment George made up a somewhat unlikely story of having hunted the horse the day before and the box having broken down. However the animal finally arrived, and the client rode it, but did not think it was quite what he wanted. While they all went into the house the horse box drove off taking the horse back to Tom's yard. Just as I arrived for lunch the client was saying goodbye, and – consternation – remarked that he was going to look at a horse at Dr Connors' place that afternoon. George hurried off to telephone Tom to tell him at all costs to hide the horse as the possible buyer had already tried it.

Ronnie Marmont is without doubt the best dressed horse coper – very dandified – he also is a past master at turning his horses out. One summer I rode Cufflink and Rajah for him at several shows, and they always looked wonderful. Ronnie impressed on me that he did not mind at all if we won or not, which I must admit I did not believe, but the horses were both so perfect that they always did win.

The first occasion I rode Cufflink was in the lightweight class at Richmond, judged by the Duke of Beaufort. Before we went in I asked Ronnie what happened when I had to run the horse up – 'Just watch what the one before you does', he told me. Well, Cufflink was pulled in first! When Ronnie came into the ring acting groom, with rubber and brush, I asked, 'Now what do I do?' Master was walking down the line of horses looking at each one, so Ronnie proceeded to do a splendid cabaret turn. He stepped out in front of the horses and mimed walking an imaginary horse down, with his right hand holding an imaginary rein with two fingers, he then turned and minced back. The few people in the stand were rolling about he was so funny.

Whenever I met him, Ronnie always had some fabulous hunter which he was on the point of getting, and which was absolutely made for me; but like the Campbells his horses were always coming but never arrived!

Talking of horse dealing – not so long ago a dealer in Leicestershire sold two horses to another dealer in Yorkshire. The horses had only just arrived in the Yorkshireman's yard, when he was rung up from a dealer in the south who was desperate to buy two horses fit to go out hunting at once, for two Americans who had come over unexpectedly. After only a brief respite in Yorkshire off trundled the horses to the south, where they were instantly boxed up again and sent up to the meet of the Cottesmore. The two Americans duly appeared mounted on these much travelled animals, to the astonishment of the Leicestershire dealer who was out hunting and recognised them as the ones he had just sent up north. When he asked the Americans what they were riding, they told him that the dealer in the south had bought both horses for them in the autumn, and had been keeping them at their expense ever since. They had wired him two days before their appearance!

11

BECOMING
JOINT MASTER

In 1959 I became Joint Master with Tony for one year, before he left (on May 1st), returned to Gumley, and took the Fernie hounds.

George Barker retired in '59 and we put Jack Littleworth on as Huntsman. He had whipped in to the Quorn since the war, and was without doubt one of the best whippers-in there has ever been. He was a great man across country and a superb and sympathetic horseman. Although he was very good with hounds (he loved them and they certainly loved him) he never excelled as a huntsman; perhaps he had whipped-in too long, but more likely it was because he was a sick man.

Although he was suffering from an ulcer all the time that I knew him, Jack was always keen to go on hunting till dark. He never wore a watch and seemed amazed when one suggested going home. One day we were on the very top of Charnwood, by Timber Wood at three o'clock in a blinding snow storm. Everyone else had wisely gone home, bar the Hunt servants, the secretary and me. Jack asked me what I would like to do next; when I said, 'Go home', he seemed very concerned and asked if I was not feeling well.

After a season or so, one of our chief difficulties was to persuade Jack ever to get rid of a single hound. However ugly it might be, he would say belligerently that he or she would hunt; and if a young dog or bitch did not enter Jack was positive that it would hunt like mad the next time out. One must be ruthless with a pack of hounds, keep only the good ones, certainly in work if not in looks. Bad habits are very catching and a hound that is not good in its work can let the whole pack down.

After George Barker retired, I quite often used to go and have tea with him and Mrs Barker. George knew the whole Quorn country like the back of his hand – every field and hedge row, almost every blade of grass. If I told him we had had a good hunt from some covert, but was not sure where we had been, George could work it out exactly. 'Did you go over the brook or right handed?' he would ask, 'You must have jumped some rails in the corner by a hovel – then down a hill to a fence with a big ditch towards you at the bottom – I expect hounds ran through that little spinney on your left, and across the lane,' and so on.

George had many entrancing stories of the old days, which I could, and often did, listen to for hours. He told me how Phillip Hubbersty offered a rather surly man on the road a florin to shut the gate, (2/- or ten pence in case you do not know, and generous at the time.) saying 'Have a drink with me'. 'I don't drink,' the man said. 'Well have a smoke then.' 'I don't smoke.' 'If I give you this,' Phillip asked 'What will you do with it?' 'Put it in the plate at chapel.' 'You won't you know,' Phillip remarked, putting the coin back in his pocket.

One story which George did not tell me himself, was when he had a day visiting another pack of hounds, hunted by an amateur. George, always anxious to help, and getting rather impatient with the slowness of the proceedings, began to cheer hounds on, and was heard calling 'On, on, on you slow old dog hounds,' which obviously did not please the master-huntsman excessively.

The hunt ball used to be held on a Friday night at Quenby, on condition that I left my dinner party and arrived early to receive the guests with Sir Harold and Lady Nutting. One year, soon after I became joint master, we had been hunting in the area that day and lost a couple of hounds. On the way back to Quenby, by myself, I met Vision trotting down the road through Baggrave Park. With a proprietary interest in 'my hounds' I was determined to catch her, which I succeeded in doing after about the fifth attempt, in the head lights of my car. I was dressed in a very chic long, tight, slinky green satin dress, and Vision tried to dive between my legs, which was quite impractical due to the long, tight, slinky green dress! With the result that I fell flat on my face on the road.

When I finally arrived at Quenby, I was covered in mud, and a little blood, and was not nearly so soignée as when I set out. But Vision was safely in the car, where she remained during the ball. The rest of the night she spent in a loose box at Gaddesby, where she howled without ceasing and kept everyone awake. When I fetched her in the morning she growled at me (after all we had been through) as I deposited her back at the kennels Jack said, 'I wish you had got the other young bitch who is missing, Vision would have found her own way home.' There is gratitude for you!

Tim Llewellen-Palmer, who got on very well with all the farmers, joined me as joint master in 1960, and stayed for two years, until he got married and returned to Wiltshire. Eric Crosfield was joint master also for those two years, and helped enormously financially. He had hunted from Melton for years but when he married Joan Balding, they moved to Ashby Pastures. Joan renovated the Farm House at Cream Gorse where she lives now, and her farm is great fun to ride over.

Brigadier Dolly Tilney took Tim's place in '62. He was Field Master on Mondays and Fridays, but otherwise left me to run the kennels and stables, and look after the Tuesday–Saturday country. We each provided horses for the Hunt servants.

I made an unfortunate error at one of the first meets after Dolly joined me. On seeing his wife, Fanny, I rode up to speak to her, but to my astonishment she turned and fled into the house, and did not appear again. Afterwards it was explained that she was terrified of horses, and that I was on no account to go near her when mounted.

It was about this time that I realised that breeding a pack of hounds is not without complications, and on learning that it takes one year to ruin a pack of hounds, but ten to put them right again, I thought that help was needed. Fortunately Ronnie Wallace came to the rescue, offering his advice which was invaluable, and has certainly paid off and improved our hounds. He has continued to advise on our breeding ever since.

Dolly Tilney used to get tired or perhaps bored by mid afternoon, and would say to me that he was sure I could cope, because he was going home. Then sweeping off his cap he would say, 'Goodnight'. The first few times that this happened everyone thought that hounds were going home, so they went too, consequently we had some very jolly hunts with hardly anyone left out with us, much to the annoyance of those who had gone home therefore missing the fun. Eventually no one dared leave until hounds were safely in their hound van.

David Keith had already arranged to come in joint with Dolly and me for the next season, when in February 1965 Dolly had his very bad fall, from which he has never fully recovered. What a tragic accident.

David and I had a very happy mastership together from '65 until '72 when he retired after breaking his leg very badly. David took a great interest in hounds, and their breeding, and judged many puppy shows as well as at Peterborough.

Early in the season of '67 Jack Littleworth, who had suffered from an ulcer for some time, went into hospital and was found to have a tumour on the brain. Although he was able to return to the kennels after an operation, and was technically in charge, he was not allowed to ride. Michael Farrin who had been our First Whipper-in since '62, therefore hunted hounds, which he did extremely well.

The doctors told David and me that Jack could never hunt again, so we had an exceedingly important decision to make – who to put on. In actual fact there was never any doubt in our minds. If we looked for a new huntsman we should try to find some one exactly like Michael – he crossed the country with consumate ease, was a very fine horseman, and certainly had a flair for hunting the fox. His only possible disadvantage was his youth, he was just 25 but time would undoubtedly alter this! and he was unmarried, supposedly a handicap for a huntsman. (This was rectified in '69 when he married Gill Cleave at one of the most enjoyable weddings I have ever attended.)

Our decision has certainly proved an outstanding success.

When David Keith resigned, the Quorn were in a difficult position, as I could not go on alone. (Just imagine trying to cope with a Monday Field on Muxlow Hill!)

There did not seem to be anyone suitable, capable, or willing to take the job. Fred Barker was obviously an ideal choice, but he had many commitments already. Venetia Barker, his wife, had been hunting with the Quorn for four or five years, looking very elegant, always beautifully turned out side saddle. Fred had only been hunting regularly with us for the past two seasons. His father and mother had both been Master of the VWH, and his aunt, Effie Parker, Master of the Garth for years, with her father (Fred's grandfather) before her.

It seemed a remote chance that Fred would accept, as he was chairman of a big helicopter firm, which was time consuming and entailed many trips abroad, as well as running a stud farm, and farming land in Wiltshire. Anyhow it was worth trying. It so happened that Fred and Venetia landed in his helicopter in my field before a meet at Barsby; he had hardly stepped out of his helicopter before I put the question to him. To my relief he did not turn it down, but said that he would think it over and talk to his father.

My next step was to contact the chairman, Mike Crawshaw, as in fact it was up to him and the committee to arrange the mastership. Finding Mike was easier said than done, as he was on his way to Paris. Finally I thought I had caught up with him (by telephone) at Whites – but no – only a cryptic message about Lord Crawshaw having no passport, which would seem to have nothing to do with me, and that he would ring me from Heathrow; which he duly did. Whether it was the noise of the airport, the bad line, or the fact that Mike had undoubtedly lunched very well; he could not hear a word I said.

Afterwards, I gather, in the aeroplane, he told Norman Johnstone that the call had been very important, 'I am appointing a master of the Quorn', he said, 'I suppose it is alright as Ulrica has fixed it – but I just wish I knew who it is.'

When Mike returned from Paris everything was sorted out, we had a committee meeting, everyone was delighted, Fred became Joint Master in '72, which was an excellent thing for the Quorn. Then in '75 James Teacher joined us.

James gives an hilarious description of his first day with the Quorn, in '59 when he was Master of the Oxford Drag. Apparently he had forgotten his top hat, so borrowed one which was several sizes too small for him and perched on the top of his head. The horse, which he had hired, had a strong disinclination to jump anything at all, and stopped with great determination and disheartening regularity at every fence; and on every single occasion James' hat fell off, so that he was obliged to dismount and pick it up. The day sounded a disaster! However, not put off, James appeared again in '62 with Bob McCreery. Wearing his own hat and riding his own horse things went much better and he became a regular with the Quorn, and no one enjoyed it more.

After James married Chloe they both hunted with us on Mondays and Fridays, motoring up from Kent. When he became Joint Master he and Chloe bought Carlton Lodge, next door to me; they bought some land with the house, which is all grass with nice fences. A few chickens are kept at Carlton Lodge which are much appreciated by the foxes who live in my garden!

12

MAUDIE

I suppose Maudie was one of the best-known dogs in the County. When Migs Greenall's golden retriever had a litter of puppies Migs gave me one; and for twelve years Maudie accompanied me everywhere. She never missed any festivities from point to points and shows to committee meetings and dinner parties.

She shared my dislike for late nights and was adept at 'making a move'! After dinner when she was sound asleep at my feet, I only had to whisper 'home' and she would spring up, hurry round saying goodbye to everyone and then stand by the door looking back at me expectantly. 'What does she want?' someone would ask. 'She wants to go home.' It was a sure way to break up a party.

In our own house when she thought it was bed time, Maudie would go and stand in front of any guest, staring fixedly at them, and willing them to leave.

She was a dedicated foxhunter; when she was very young I took her cubhunting with me in the early part of the season when we were 'holding up'. She would never leave my horse's side until she saw or heard a fox, when she would dash to the covert to turn it back, before returning to me. She was a great help until she became a bit too keen and thought that she must continue hunting the fox, so that one morning I saw the fox closely pursued by Maudie, followed by the Quorn hounds!

Every season the Miss Hepplewhites used to let her follow with them on Tuesdays, and sometimes on Saturdays. The Miss Hepplewhites have followed the Quorn on bicycles, car, and foot for many years and never miss a day. Maudie used to adore her days with them, and got very excited when she saw a fox. When I drove up to the place where we were unboxing, Maudie would leap out of my car and rush off without a backward glance, to find the Miss Hepplewhites.

On Fridays near Gaddesby she used to come out with Gordon and Mrs Pick. On one occasion at Cream Gorse when Maudie was in the back of the land rover, she saw the fox go away, so out she jumped and coursed it to Ashby Pastures (6 or 7 fields). When it reached the wood Maudie turned and trotted back, very out of breath, to the land rover. Luckily at the time Michael was still in Cream Gorse with hounds; as he always seems to think 'cur dogs' spoil a hunt. When hounds came out on the line of Maudie's fox I said to James, 'Don't tell Michael about Maudie.' In the event the fox had been so demoralised by Maudie that hounds caught it directly they got into the Pastures. James could not resist saying to the huntsman, 'I believe a dog chased the fox.' At which Michael said, 'I know, and I know exactly whose dog it was too.'

Maudie had a phobia that she could not bear anyone except me to hold her on a lead. At Fred's first hedge cutting event, his speech was made very much more difficult by Maudie standing and barking furiously because she could not get to me. Poor Fred had to shout to be heard.

At one of the horse sales at the Repository in Leicester I said to Rick Lawson, 'Hold Maudie a moment I must go to the loo.' Within a few minutes there was the most frightful commotion in the rather crowded 'Ladies' as Maudie tore in backwards, with a very determined expression and her collar half off, and a very red-faced Rick on the other end of the lead being dragged in. On the same day she leaped about three feet in the air and cleverly snatched a piece of pork pie out of a completely strange man's hand, which he was on the point of putting in his mouth. The man gave me a withering glance saying, 'If she is that hungry she better have it.' Maudie was delighted, but I felt that he might report me to the RSPCA!

When I was trying a beautiful grey horse at Robin Leyland's, as I rode round the meadow I asked Robin to let my dog go. She was so relieved to be free that she sped to me and jumped up against the horse's hind quarters, which astonished and definitely annoyed the grey horse. Even Robin seemed quite put out and asked if Maudie always behaved like that. I told him it was essential to find out if an animal was good with hounds.

At the present time I have a Rhodesian Ridge back, Simba, who is very ferocious with anyone who is frightened of him, but not so brave with people who are not. He will stand and bark looking tremendously threatening at the gate, but if some tactless character takes no notice but comes in, Simba hurries back into the house growling to himself. To give him confidence I am thinking of putting a notice on the gate, 'guard dog patrolling – survivors will be prosecuted.'

Simba and I were very proud at the terrier show run by

the Hunt supporters, as we won the dog most like its owner – our wrinkled foreheads we thought . . .

The only person who treats Simba with due respect is the Editor of *Horse and Hound*.

13

ACCIDENTS

When Alan Whicker was making a film of the Quorn he told me afterwards that he could not see that it was cruel to the fox, but he did think that it was terribly cruel to the people who rode to hounds. 'Leicestershire seemed to echo with the dull crack of breaking bones.'

I have broken quite a few myself, and came to know the pay bed wing at the Nottingham General Hospital rather too well, at one time.

I think most of the bad falls I have had have been due to bogs, usually landing in one. When the bigger and better a horse has jumped, the more likely he is to stand on his head or turn a somersault when his front feet are firmly stuck in the mud.

On one occasion when there was boggy ground in front of some rails, my animal failed to get her feet out to take off, falling and then treading all over me getting up, and so breaking my leg. The Duke of Beaufort had broken his leg fishing the year before, and had had a special stirrup iron made big enough to take a plaster, so that he could hunt. He very kindly lent this to me, and as my plaster only went up to my knee, I was able to ride and hunt in comparative comfort.

I broke vertebrae twice. The first time I wore a sort of plaster barrel round my middle, which entailed buying a maternity dress to cover it, and which does nothing for one's morale. The second time the break was between my shoulder blades, so plaster was out of the question, and I just lived on dope. Fortunately, at this time I had the most wonderful old horse, given to me by Terry Skinner, called Top Brass, who was an absolute patent safety. So I was able to go out hunting on him for an hour or so, fortified by masses of pain-killers swallowed down with neat whisky. It was better than staying at home!

I am always frightfully disagreeable when in hospital so that my friends dread coming to see me. When she broke her neck, Maggy Myddelton was simply wonderful – she was so cheerful. She sat bolt upright, looking rather like Buddha, with a crown over her head, with steel rods from it literally driven into her head, holding it absolutely fixed to the plaster below. I found it incomprehensible how cheerful she was, in that awful position.

Maggy has sadly since her accident had to give up hunting with us, but Rid, her husband, still comes all the way from Chirk Castle in Wales, to hunt on Mondays.

Riding in an Oxford Grind some 25 years ago Mike Crawshaw had the most terrible fall, which left him completely paralysed from the waist down. Despite this he does much work in the County, sits in the House of Lords, helps with Riding for the Disabled and other charities. He shoots from a land rover, and he comes out hunting, using a special saddle, but dressed in proper hunting clothes, scarlet coat and all. He has no feeling in his legs, so a few months ago when he had a fall from his horse, he broke his leg, without knowing it; now his leg has set itself crooked.

14

FIELD
MASTERS

The huntsman does his best to provide sport, and to help him the field master tries to prevent the pack being over-ridden; so there must be a clear understanding between the two. It is not an easy job to control a large and eager field; it requires tact, firmness, and knowledge of the country.

If you have a professional huntsman then at least when things go wrong you will only get an acid look – if you have the misfortune to act for an amateur huntsman you will find yourself on the receiving end of some fairly virulent abuse. In my experience amateur huntsmen are quite incapable of saying anything in the hunting field without prefacing it with an unprintable adjective.

I think it is unfair to compare the modern field masters with characters before the war. In those days a fast horse to gallop and jump was the first essential, secondly a loud and commanding voice. It has certainly become a much more difficult task in recent years. Nowadays, you must know where you are; and what is more, if possible where you are going, which is quite a problem since you do not know what the fox has in mind!

A certain knowledge of farming is very important these days, and modern methods do not make things easy. Direct drilling, or fields that are under sewn, are not so obvious as a brown ploughed field with little green shoots coming up! I asked once if a field was drilled, and was told that it had been 'scuffled' which got me nowhere; as I had no idea if one did or did not ride over 'scuffled' land.

Before the day's hunting it is essential to find out where there are in-calf heifers which should be left in complete peace and quiet, or very pregnant ewes.

Very few people seem to look at hounds, but they become mesmerised by jumping fences, and will after-wards say that they have had a splendid hunt if they have jumped a dozen or so obstacles. It does not appear to register with them whether hounds were running, or the huntsman was casting on, or even drawing for an outlier.

If hounds double back you will meet folk riding des-perately in the opposite direction, as though it was a paper chase, or as if they would be disqualified if they did not go the exact way the rider in front had gone. Perhaps it is just fear of missing out one single jump that could have been taken.

One memorable day when James Teacher was first acting field master on a Friday, he was run away with in Baggrave Park. He went flat out right round the outside of the Park, and then round again and again in ever-diminishing circles, followed every yard of the way by 80 per cent of our very large field (over ever-diminishing fences!) Apparently they were all enchanted and thought it a magnificent hunt. The remaining few of us had a very enjoyable little hunt unhampered by any followers. I thought this the ideal way of coping with a big crowd and suggested that James should repeat the manoeuvre on other days, but he has selfishly refused to do so.

It has been repeated so often that I am sick of hearing, that Algy Burnaby told the pretty ladies to hold hard and the ugly ones could go on. But I do think it worth telling of an incident when Tony was Master of the Quorn, and several of our hardest riding females had all just had babies. I suddenly heard Tony in stern tones shout, 'Will the nursing mothers please hold hard.' Urkie Newton, Migs Greenall and Stella Molony were certainly three of them, but I am sure there were others. Anyhow they pulled up very smartly!

There is no doubt at all that masters were far fiercer before the war than they are at the present time; subscribers held them in great awe, which I do not find the case now! Hunting was far more regimented and I think there is a happier more relaxed atmosphere today. Pre-war everyone had to be at the meet on time, properly turned out. You would have been in trouble if you wandered up later to join in, (that is – if you were caught).

It is difficult for a field master today to give hounds the room they used to have, because if you give them too much of a start, then have to circumvent some wheat or seeds you may get left too far behind to catch up. Certainly hounds are ridden on, with all the Leicestershire packs, more than would ever have been allowed in the old days. You often see hounds practically surrounded, with people ahead of them on each flank, then the fox, headed, turns back; I think on these occasions it must be very hard for a Huntsman to keep his temper. Of course if he happens to be an amateur, the answer is that he does not.

I find it a pity that riders, when they have 'jumped the gun' are no longer made to come back over the fence they have just negotiated – it used to be highly entertaining to watch the return, when the fence happened to have a drop and a big ditch, which had to be taken the other way.

I once told Geoffrey Bevan to jump back, but he just laughed!

There was one young man who always fell off from fright, whenever Tony told him to hold hard, long before he even got to the fence.

It was entirely my invention that lady masters should wear gold buttons. I had no wish to wear a scarlet coat, as I had a terrible feeling that I might look like the 'Tally Ho Band!' but one obviously wants to be easily recognised as a master. (I get knocked about quite enough as it is). I went to Mr Green at Frank Hall's in Market Harborough, who was rather disapproving of the idea at first, but made me a very smart coat, and then agreed it looked very good. He promised not to let anyone but a master have gold buttons on their coat. I think most lady masters have since copied my invention. I think there should be four buttons on the front, and two at the back.

15

THE SECRETARY
AND OTHERS

The job of secretary is arduous and never-ending (or should be!). He, like the master, ought to attend all the local functions to do with hunting or farming. (No need to attend the church fete!)

On a hunting day the master will arrange which way he wants to draw with the huntsman, then he or the secretary must go round and warn the farmers and landowners that hounds may be over their land, and find out where any snags are, such as in lamb ewes and in calf heifers. After the day's hunting if anyone is angry for some reason or other, the secretary must hurry off to try to pacify them.

We were very lucky when Jonathan Inglesant left in '76 to have Charley Humfrey to take his place; it was a great advantage that he had hunted with us for some years, so knew the country and many of the farmers.

Going round seeing people, one comes across some odd characters, as well as many very nice ones. Last season we were trying to open up a piece of country we had not been in for some years; Charley, the secretary, Michael, the huntsman, and I went to investigate with

Geoff Brooks who farms in that vicinity. We called on a rather strange man, who had only recently moved in. When we asked him if we might draw his wood he replied, 'What with a paint brush and easel?'. He then inquired what there was 'in it' for him. We decided that we were not quite on the same wave length, and there seemed no future there, so we left.

The secretary is employed by the committee and not by the masters. It is his job to extort money from the subscribers, and see that no one comes out who has not paid. It is also up to him to arrange the fencing and damage.

Jeff Pick, our fence mender is invaluable; he knows everyone, and I should think knows just about every fence in the Quorn country. I must admit there are times when he is not so popular, when riders have made for a place where they know there is a gap, only to find a formidable post and rails in its place. Jeff and his mate waste no time in mending any holes the moment we have gone.

The huntsman, apart from looking after the hounds, is one of the most important ambassadors of the Hunt. He keeps in touch with the keepers and farmers to find out where the foxes are likely to be, or if foxes have been doing any damage. He sends out stopping cards, so that the earths and drains are stopped before we come hunting. He also arranges the Keepers' Dinner, a very important function.

A very big item in the running of the kennels is picking up flesh. This is not only to feed the hounds, but does a very important service in the country. If a horse or cow, or even a sheep or young calf dies on a farm, they ring up the kennels and it is fetched. Our pick-up truck seems to be permanently on the road.

In the summer I know Michael tries to see most of the

farmers, many while he is out hound exercise, others he calls in to see. In this way he finds out, not only where litters of cubs have been born, but where kale and roots are being planted which will be useful to draw. It can be very handy in the coming season if he knows where a new gate has been put in, or an old one blocked up, and where a ride has become completely overgrown. He calls round to see the puppies out at walk, and he has to try to find new walks, as many homes where they used to walk puppies now have dangerous roads too near for safety. It is far better for the young hounds if they can roam about loose; they do not learn anything if they are shut in a kennel.

The Puppy Show entails a great deal of work as the kennels have to look spotless, the railings painted, the lawns mown, and of course the young entry looking their best. I recall once when showing the hounds to another master the week before our Puppy Show, he threw his cigarette end down on the gravel, and the huntsman, who was then Jack Littleworth, stepped forward and picked it up.

On a normal hunting day Michael Farrin begins his day in kennels at 6.30 a.m. when he feeds all hounds that are not going hunting, sees to any lame ones, then walks out the rest of the hounds before his breakfast, which is about 8.30. After that there is usually some telephoning, and he has to change into his hunting clothes. The kennelman and 1st whipper-in load up hounds, which Michael has drawn the day before, and the 1st whipper-in, Tony Wright, drives the hound van. On Tuesdays and Saturdays when we only have one horse, Michael drives the horse box.

When Michael came to us as 1st Whipper-in from the North Cotswold, Brian Parry the Master there, was having a sale of the Hunt horses. Michael told me that two of the hunters which he had ridden his last season there, were really good, and worth buying; so I went to the sale at Leicester and bought Maverick for £300. When we got him back to the kennels I must admit I thought I was mad to have paid that price for a small cobby animal! Michael then proceeded to ride him for twelve seasons with the Quorn, originally on the Mondays and Fridays, later when he was hunting hounds, and Maverick was getting older, he took him Tuesdays and Saturdays. Michael has counted up from his diary that in the thirteen years he hunted Maverick on 357 days. I will remember one day out cubhunting, when hounds ran fast and well, some strangers happily followed Michael, thinking that Maverick was a cubhunting pony, but were quickly disillusioned, and baffled, when Michael popped over some awe inspiring obstacles.

We gave Maverick to Michael's sister Jo in '74 when we thought he was no longer up to being a huntsman's horse, she hunted him for four seasons, and he was finally put down in '78 at the age of twenty-two.

About the best horse Michael says he has ever ridden was General Gordon, who was bought for him by Fred Barker when he was first Join Master. 'Gordon' had been round Badminton, he certainly jumped in magnificent style, and was a lovely tall horse.

He now has a superb horse to ride in Colonius by Colonist, very kindly lent to me by the Queen Mother. Colonius had won six 3-mile chases, and been in training all his life, but he took to hunting straight away, jumping anything he meets with obvious enjoyment.

16

THE TUESDAY
SATURDAY
COUNTRY

Of all the week, I think that I enjoy my Tuesdays and Saturdays most – they have a quite different atmosphere to the Monday–Fridays. There are fewer people, and they are farmers and local people (who enjoy watching hounds work) and, although they thoroughly enjoy a good hunt, they never seem bored on a poor day.

The country varies tremendously, the Tuesdays being wilder, with stone walls to jump, bracken (which is very high and green in the autumn), rocks, and woodland.

The Saturdays cover a large area of which some is lovely country and well fenced, some plough, and a few big woods.

On the Monday–Friday side one can easily jump 50 to 80 fences in the day; on a Saturday we would not go over anything like that number, but what you do meet you have to jump, if you want to be with hounds. You need a very good and clever horse as the obstacles can be big and very awkward. I love it on the 'unfashionable side'! The dog hounds are wonderful to see and hear when they tear across the country in full cry, with their gorgeous deep voices, or when they work out a scentless line with great perseverance, never giving up.

In 1977 we had a marvellous hunt with a mixed pack of 21½ couple. We had met at the Bull's Head, Grace Dieu on Tuesday 8 March and hunted around there until we found a really good fox in Dry Brook, (opposite the Monastery). Hounds hunted him back over Sharpley, which is very rough going, bracken, rocks, with stone walls; leaving Cademan on their left they ran through Grace Dieu, which is a wood with very overgrown, deep muddy rides. Coming away from here by Manor Farm hounds checked. Friction, a first season bitch by Heythrop Footman '71, was the only one who could own the line over a very foiled field to the main Ashby Road. Once over the 'turn pike' hounds ran on well down the Grace Dieu brook, swinging left across Hall Farm, Osgathorpe, over the Belton Road by the Gate Inn and on to Barrow Hill. By now we were in Saturday Country, mostly grass, with fly fences and timber. A useful Holloa came from the road, just as hounds had checked for a moment, and they were on again, leaving Stordon Grange on their right, they ran very fast to Thringston and up the valley to Swannington. Still running hard they crossed the railway line and road into Atherstone Country by Sinope, then turned right short of Ravenstone. The pack ran parallel with the main road by Alton Grange towards Packington, where they turned short of the village and coursed their fox back to Alton Grange Wood where the very tired fox got to ground just in front of hounds. This was a very good hound hunt of over 17 miles with two points of 5½ and 4½ miles in 2 hours 10 minutes.

One of the fascinating aspects of foxhunting is the unexpected – so often there can be a super hunt from a bad meet or from a covert hardly considered worth drawing. Or some days the weather makes you wish you had stayed in bed, (well – almost!) and then suddenly you enjoy yourself madly. And of course vice versa – the best meet can prove terribly disappointing.

I find it the most lovely surprise when we run into the Monday country on a Saturday – well, to be truthful it is always lovely if we do, but not always a surprise! But it is glorious to be able to enjoy the cream of Leicestershire with only about twenty people participating. I remember rushing back in great excitement one Saturday evening to telephone Fred, asking him 'Guess where we finished up today – Upper Broughton Station.'

One very good hunt was written up by Jonathan Inglesant, from plough to the best of the Monday Country. I shall quote him:

QUORN DOG HOUNDS
HIT TOP FORM

Whether a hunt is great or not, is of course, a matter of opinion, but the run that followed the Quorn's meet at Remstone Hall on January 8th ('72) needs no embellishing from me. For those who know the country the facts will speak for themselves. Finding at just after 1 p.m. in Hoton New Covert the doghounds hunted their fox away to the brook. Turning right along the brook – and finding all the earths well stopped – the fox crossed back and ran right handed to where he was found. Hounds quickly picked up his line, and ran towards Hoton village, but swung right, short of the Nottingham road, at King's Bridge. Leaving Remstone on the left the fox crossed the Wymeswold road and ran on to Peasland. Hounds worked out his line over the plough, crossed the Wysall lane, and hitting the grass, really sung to his scent. Leaving Thorpe-in-the-Glebe on the left they went through the corner of Triangle Spinner; crossed the brook with Willoughby Gorse on the right, and were quickly over the road and the site of the Battle of Willoughby Field. Crossing the Widmerpool lane nearly to the Fosse, hounds turned left, the tired fox now starting to jink about. He ran round Widmerpool village to the station lane where he doubled back. This was his farthest point – roughly 6 miles. Hounds hunted him into Flint Hills where he got to ground. This had been the doghounds at their best, having to work every inch of the way and covering what must be as fine and varied a line of country as one could find.

17

THE QUORN
NOW

It is interesting to see how the Hunt Servants who have been with the Quorn have fared since. Peter Wright, who was 2nd Whipper-in when Jack Littleworth was Huntsman, hunts the Cottesmore now; while Jimmy Laing who was our next 2nd Whipper-in has hunted the Burton since 1967. I remember when Jimmy was coming to us from the Meynell I asked Dermot Kelly, the Master, if he had a good holloa, to which Dermot looked superior and said 'I've simply no idea, we don't have anyone holloaing with my hounds.' 'Do you mean everyone whistles?' I asked, 'It must sound like Waterloo Station.'

At that time Denis Boyles was our first Whipper-in; now he hunts the Devon and Somerset Stag Hounds.

Lionel Salter, 1st Whipper-in to Michael, hunts the Buccleuch, and Chris Bowld who followed Lionel went recently as kennel Huntsman to Brian Fanshawe with the North Cotswold, while Tony Wright who was our 2nd Whipper-in, took Chris' place with us.

If the kennels and stables are on friendly terms, or at any rate on speaking terms, it is a great advantage. In days gone by I have not only had to order the horses, but remember to say that the huntsman would like a standing martingale or a different bridle. Now fortunately all is well, the Stud Groom, Peter Houghton, turns the hunters out to perfection without being reminded of anything, and they are well exercised and very fit.

The only superstition I have, in which I believe implicitly, is that if you have a keeper off and a strap flapping you will have a fall. My father told me this, explaining that it made sense, as if you were careless enough to have your bridle improperly put on, you were careless enough to have a fall. Luckily my bridles are fixed correctly these days; but in the past I have been obliged to pull up between fences to anchor a loose end! I would not dream of riding down the road even, with a keeper off, my horse might trip, you never know.

Some years ago when we unboxed the horses, one had been sent out with neither stirrups nor leathers on the saddle. I thought it was quite funny until I noticed that the horse in question was mine. Luckily we were meeting with Frank Hewitt at Old Parks Farm so there was no problem.

Foxhunting attracts a great variety of people, and this certainly applies to the Quorn – well if I am going to do some name-dropping, I shall start by dropping the biggest name of all – The Prince of Wales – who comes out with us quite often, accompanied by Sir John Miller, the Crown Equery, who has hunted with the Quorn for many years, driving from Windsor, London, or Sandringham. No one seems happier out with hounds than Prince Charles; not only does he obviously love jumping large fences, which he accomplishes in great style, but he enjoys watching hounds work, and appreciates the opportunity of spending a day in the country. He takes a far greater and more intelligent interest in what is going on than most of our followers do. He has a friendly word for everyone, whether they are on a horse or on foot, so that it is a great asset to have His Royal Highness out with us. I think the 'Windsor' coat he wears, royal blue with red collar and cuffs, is very smart. I believe the last person to hunt in the Windsor coat was King George III.

Who else to mention? Chris Collins who won many steeple chases and was leading amateur and has represented this country eventing. Dick Hern and Barry Hills, top trainers, who both have a great go. Jockey, Willie Carson, who on one occasion was mistaken for my son! (Well if I had a son I would quite like him to be Champion Jockey!). MP Marcus Kimball who does so much for the Field Sports Society. Ex MP and Labour peer, Lord Paget, whose father, Guy Paget wrote many hunting books, and whose ambition it is to be killed out hunting, as indeed his father was.

Those in the hunting field change as the years roll by, and there are few subscribers now, who were hunting before the war. Pat Weldon, Urkie Newton, Arthur Gemmell, and George Coombes, who used to farm and now runs a livery yard. He is the only man I know who still hunts six days a week, with at least three packs, at the present time, as he always did. When hunting is finally over he hurries to Ireland where he buys young horses to make in the summer.

Then of course the Miss Hepplewhites have been foot followers with the Quorn since well before the war. They and some others who come out in cars do know what they are doing; but it is a pity that the majority seem quite unable to keep quiet, but must leap into their motor cars at the first sound they hear and roar off. It appears to be a sort of treasure hunt to some folk, the point being to see the fox, and of course to yell their heads off if they do.

They spoil many hunts, while if they only remained still and quiet, they would do less harm and see much more.

I believe practically all hunts have supporters clubs now; they came into being after the war, and the enormous number of members all over the country show what a tremendous enthusiasm there is for foxhunting.

Our Supporters Club was started in '60. Bill Headley, whom I first met in Palestine in the war when he was District Commissioner, is the chairman, and Pat Bull the secretary. They run many jolly evenings, a very good supper, with entertaining speeches to follow, a dance and a barbecue and various money making affairs; from which they have presented the Hunt, over the years, with a hound van, two pick-up trucks, the secretary's van, hound benches, and water bowls in the stables.

A quite new venture which has become very popular in the last few years is the Team Cross Country Race. Teams of usually four, go round a course of two or three miles, and the first three to finish count, the fastest time winning.

These events are entertaining for the public, as a team goes every five minutes, so there is never a dull pause, and as a rule there are spectactular falls. If the prize money is sponsored and the day fine, a great deal of money can be made.

The first season or so teams entered for a jolly ride round, but it has now become very professional, and it has been known for a fancied team to have a breakdown en route thus enabling them to go last and to know what time they have to beat. At our Quorn event one year, two of the top winning teams were each short of riders, so they amalgamated. The result was riveting – at the third fence there was complete shambles and one rider was knocked down. I heard a flow of abuse and bad language, then two of one team raced on, while the other two galloped back to their horse box still cursing.

We have a lovely course, both to ride or watch, on Muxlow Hill. It is very well organised by Geoff and Gale Brooks; there are many sponsors including the Playboy Club.

One festivity which is unique to the Quorn is Fred Barker's Jumping Show, which is held in the Oxby's indoor riding school at Kinoulton each March. It is a marvellous party given by Fred and organised by Margaret and Denzil Oxby, the latter building the course. It starts at 6.30 p.m. and ends about 11, with ten teams of four jumping two rounds each. Among the teams are two farmers' teams, another consisting of their wives, a team of the kennel staff, one of girl grooms, and the Master's team (we three and the Huntsman). Farmers and other friends are invited to come and watch and drink delicious hot spiced red wine, or anything else they fancy. The whole evening is hilarious, and by the second round quite a number of the competitors take the wronge course, which appears almost impossible to do! Riders and spectators alike are in very good form indeed.

Before the war farmers were given lunch in a marquee at the point to point, now that this is not feasible, they are given free car park passes. Our point to point is held at the end of April at Garthorpe, the Melton Hunt Club course, which has permanent buildings, and is a good course to see. Henry Barton, helped by John Smith runs our meeting, which usually makes a good sum of money and has very good racing.

The Quorn has always relied on outsiders for much of its income, but in this present day and age, we have had to limit the number of subscribers who do not live in the country; as too many people not only spoil the sport, but we felt that a vast, and possibly unruly crowd riding over their land, was not fair to the farmers, who by and large give us such a warm welcome.

A new feature of the foxhunting scene is the entertainment and hospitality given to the farmers by the subscribers, as well as by the Hunt. I am sure that this does a great deal of good. We have dinners every season, one for each part of the country; the Monday Farmers' Dinner, the Tuesday Farmers' Dinner and so on.

David and Caroline Keith used to invite thirty or forty farmers with their wives to their home in Norfolk each summer, show them round David's farm, and give them a huge lunch. Fred Barker has carried on the tradition and yearly he and Venetia give a sumptious lunch party at Lushill where there is the stud to look at, as well as the farm and lovely garden.

As James Teacher lives in Kent it is too far for him to invite the farmers for lunch; but it is a very big house so no doubt he and Chloe are planning a vast weekend party!

Our Chairman, Lord Crawshaw, and some MPs led by Stephen Hastings arrange a lunch at the House of Commons for about forty farmers and wives, who go to London by coach. They can see Parliament in action (how edifying!) and visit the House of Lords. Usually the day's outing ends with tea, either at Hyde Park Barracks with the Household Cavalry, or St John's Wood with the King's Troop.

Sir John Miller, the Crown Equery often invites a coach load from one of the Melton Hunts to see round the Royal Mews and have a meal. It is fascinating to see all the horses, carriages, the State Coronation Coach, and the different harness for various ceremonial occasions.

Then the subscribers who live outside the Quorn

Country pay for a party organised by John and Rosemary Partridge, for the Monday–Friday Farmers. Last year it was a party at their lovely home at Empingham, where champagne and whisky were flowing in a very exotic marquee on the lawn; and the gardens and swimming pool (into which several people fell!) were illuminated.

There have always been a large number of hunting farmers with the Quorn, but I think at the present time there are more farming families (wives and daughters) hunting with us than ever before.

Looking back I think one remembers the good things in life and tends to forget the bad. There has certainly been a lot of fun – horses and hounds have figured largely in my life – but who would have thought when I first appeared in Leicestershire that I should one day be Joint Master of the most famous (and in my opinion the best!) pack of hounds.

The style of living has changed tremendously in my time – but then one changes oneself – age creeps on 'time's winged chariot hurries near.'

When I first hunted here I went to endless parties, and thought nothing of going to London after hunting to dance for much of the night at the Embassy Club or the Café de Paris. Now all I want is a hot bath and a drink in the company of my dog. (He does not drink, except, if he gets the chance, champagne!)

I recall in 1935 inveigling my brother Brian, who had a Spartan aeroplane, to fly to Leicestershire on a Saturday morning, which enabled me to attend the Quorn Hunt Ball on the Friday night, and then ride in a point to point in Sussex next day.

Brian reminds me that he was very cross because I had not mentioned the fact that every field, including the one in which he was to land, was ridge and furrow. As I hate small planes I was sick all the way down to Sussex, but was second in the race. The newspapers said, 'Air Girl in Horse Race.' They got it the wrong way round, it should have read, 'Horsey Girl in the Air'.

I cannot imagine at this point in time having any desire either to go to a Hunt Ball or to ride in a point to point – in fact I must confess to an overwhelming desire not to.

18

CONCLUSION

When I reflect on the difference of hunting in Leicestershire at the present time, and compare it to when I first
appeared on the scene – I think for those people who
only hunt to ride, and to jump fences, it was undoubtedly
better then, as it was all grass with not a strand of wire. I
can still hear Harold Nutting's voice of incredulous horror asking 'NO – Where?' when I remarked that I had
seen a ploughed field in the Quorn Friday country.

If you love to watch hounds – they hunt just the same
today as in our grandfather's time (I suspect better) and
they certainly have more difficulties to contend with. I
would not decry the famous names of the past, but both
huntsmen and field masters have a far trickier job to
perform today, and I would say that it is much more of a
challenge to cross the country.

Motorways and the many roads are a terrible hazard
now: but then our forbears thought that when railways
were invented that it would mean the end of hunting. In
actual fact we find some of the old disused railway lines
extremely useful, to get about on, as well as good places
to find a fox.

The expense of everything has of course rocketed. For instance in the '30s I believe it cost under £1 a week to keep a horse. The huntsman was paid £16 a month (plus house and perks) and a set of shoes for your hunter cost 6/- (30p.)

There has always been, and I hope there always will be, something magical about hunting in the Shires. Those pre-war days hold wonderful memories for me. It was an epoch I would not have missed for worlds. But one must always 'Get Forward' and I still enjoy foxhunting just as much, and am privileged to be connected with a pack of hounds and a country of which I am very proud.